Table of Contents

On Graduating from *Polyphony H.S.*: 2
   Letter from a Four-Year Submitter,
   – Emily Cutler
Made Whole: On the Nature of Poetry, ...4
   Mathematics, and How to Avoid Good-Byes
   – Clara Fannjiang
Announcing: 2010 Claudia Ann Seaman........6
   Awards for Young Writers
About the Claudia Ann Seaman Awards 7
About our Cover..8
About Us 10
Mission Belief 12
On Mutualism: The Writer and Editor...........14
   at *Polyphony H.S.* – Hedy Gutfreund
Defying Convention: The Character 16
   of vol VIII – Oly Huzenis

Epigraph, *Internal Notes from a few submitters*...17

Clara Fannjiang *Bird Under the Lamppost*........18
Raven Mathewes *Deep Sea Gigantism* 20
Rocio Guenther *Coconuts*..................................21
Emma Arett *Lady Sing the Bruise*.....................23
Madelyne Xiao *Anachronism* 25
Margaret Sullivan *Retreat, 2007* 26
Anjie Liu *Jackson Pollock* 28
Lilian Kong *Amerika* 31
Lylla Younes *Billy* 32
Stephanie Guo *Cecilia Had a Brightness*...........34
   Friday in the Speakeasy 35
   The Offering 36
John Richards *Red Line* 38
Anna Blech *Sonnet in a Stuffy Room* 40
Rachel Stone *Twenty-four* 41
   Firefly 42
Deborah Malamud *A Dead Shirt*......................43
Dylan Combs *Aurals* 44
Emily Cutler *Visiting Anna* 45
Jonah Haven *Belonging*......................................48
   The Silence that Breathing Takes................49
Peter LaBerge *Carlisle Blue* 50
   For the Fire 53
   Sailboat 54
Hannah Toke *Roots* 55
   Fleeting 56
Lila Thulin *Percussive* 60
   Honey & Vinegar 61
Julia Tompkins *When it Got Cold Out* 62
Lillian Fishman *How to Keep Your Sister's Secret*...63
   Fresh 65
   The Farm 66
Caroline Hamilton
   Wilted Grass and Interstate Lines...............67
   In the Winter..69

Rose Miles *Sulfur Dreams*.................................72
   Season of Infertile Seeds 73
Anna Feldman *This is Not a Catharsis* 74
Joanne Koong *For the Next Woman You Meet*...76
   How to Read Neruda When Heartbroken
      on a Friday Night..................................77
Lya Ferreyra *The Sanguine Sovereign* 78
Tina Zhu *Quiet is Her Favorite Fix*..................80
Raven Hogue *Yazoo City* 81
Michelle Jia *Peter Visits the Kensington Gardens* ..82
מרדת *(or Rebellious)* 85
Kathleen Cole *Running of the Children* 86
   On the Island 88
   While We Wait for Old Age 89
Phoebe Goldenberg *Red Cowboy Boots* 90
Brittany Newell *I Keep You Alive in My Dreams*..92
   Foreplay 96
   She Combs My Gnarled Hair in Record Time..98
   Traces...100
Olivia Scheyer *Dreamland Askew*....................102
Maggy Liu *The Story*.......................................104
Kevin Emery *American Soft Drink*..................108
Jordan Kincaid *For Once, Will You Respect Me* ..109
Gabriella Gonzales *Parade Ground* 111
Henry Anker *California Railroad Escape* 112
Anthony Otten *Felicity Burning* 114
Jane Ligon *Colorado* 115
Tom Costello *Platonic Rigidity* 116
   Rooftop 117
Jules Ray *In Which I Postulate*.......................118
   Searching Through the Lost and
      Found at the 21st Street Pool Hall 119
Maia Silber *Visiting Day*.................................120
Anran Yu *Heartprison* 121
Gabe Lunn *Bury Me with a Shot of Espresso* 123
Rebecca Greenberg *The Christening*.................124
Kathleen Maris *Winter*....................................127
Jack Nachmanovitch *300 Dead Blackbirds*.......128
Hayun Cho *Flight*..130
   Ghost Song...133
Katia Diamond *Come Sunday*........................135
Upasna Saha *Even You can't See*
   the Universe, Sweetheart.........................137
Sera Park *Room 201* 139
   The Report on Apricots............................140
Laura Wanamaker *Ovule* 141
Summer 2011: Images 143

Contributors' Bios 152
Editorial Staff..158
Editorial Pipeline 160

On Graduating from Polyphony H.S.: Letter from a Four-Year Submitter

I have had a passion for creative writing ever since I was a little girl. I have always loved words, and throughout my life their power has never ceased to amaze me. From the American Girl books and the *Harry Potter* series to Kathryn Stockett's *The Help* and Henrik Ibsen's *A Doll's House*, literature has given me characters to sympathize with and look up to, new ways to view the world, and things to stand up for and believe in. The world of books has always been an important part of my life, and one of my goals in life is to contribute to that world as a writer.

That's why, when I first read through a copy of *Polyphony H.S.* at a friend's house during my freshman year of high school, I knew I wanted to get involved. I had previously read some journals including one or two works by young adults each issue, but never before had I seen a literary magazine featuring quality writing by only high school students. I remember feeling shocked and delighted: here, in this magazine, were authors my own age who were creating strong characters, intricate plots, and poetic language – authors my own age whose writing moved me and would no doubt move many others. *Polyphony H.S.* gave me the chance to read works that would contribute to the world in amazing ways.

But I still hadn't even touched upon the best parts of *Polyphony H.S.* After researching the submission guidelines and revising some of my work, I submitted a short story and a poem. After a few months, I received the much-anticipated response email, opening it as my stomach flipped inside me. Not having heard much about *Polyphony H.S.*'s review process, I expected either an acceptance letter or a form rejection letter. So when I saw the word "regret," I thought I was finished reading the email. I bit my lip, trying to avert the same shaky lethargy every writer is so familiar with that comes after the word "regret."

It was only by chance that I scrolled down in the email. When I did, I became truly grateful for a magazine like *Polyphony H.S.* Because below the rejection letter was the most encouraging, thoughtful advice I had ever received as a writer. I discovered that writers and editors my own age had dedicated their time to reviewing and discussing my piece, and recording their feedback so that I could use it to improve my writing. I was overwhelmed by the amount of thought put into their comments, but at the same time, when I finished reading them, I had learned more about my writing than I could ever have imagined. The comments provided me with tangible skills I could use to revise those pieces, and more importantly, to improve all my future writings – invaluable skills such as using concrete images, thinking through line breaks to create more flow, and making sure the title is the correct one for the piece. After receiving the emails from *Polyphony H.S.*, I felt, more than ever, a part of a community of high school writers and editors. Never again would I consider *Polyphony H.S.*'s declining letters "rejection" letters. The comments both strengthened my goal to contribute to the world as a writer and reaffirmed my desire to improve my craft. And they made me want to submit again.

By now, as a recent graduate of high school, I have had the honor of appearing in *Polyphony H.S.* twice, with another piece accepted in this issue. Sometimes I look back at the magazine and think, "Really?" My work published alongside Alison Marqusee's "English," a beautiful poem that captivates not only our language but also our culture? My work published alongside Joanna Shaw's "Date a Girl Who Reads," a piece not only guaranteed to make all writers happy but also one that quenches our thirst for truly poetic language? My work published alongside Kate Bell's "My Name is Cassie, and I Will Tell You All You Need to Know About High School," a piece that masters the art of dark comedy?

I am proud and honored to be a contributor of *Polyphony H.S.* As a graduate of a high school that does not have a creative writing program, I consider *Polyphony H.S.* to have been a major learning source throughout all four years.

Next year, I plan to attend the University of Pennsylvania, where I will major in creative writing. I will miss *Polyphony H.S.* and wish to thank all writers and editors involved for their dedication. *Polyphony H.S.* has encouraged my passion for writing, strengthened my skills, and made me proud to be a writer.

Emily Cutler

Made Whole: On the Nature of Poetry, Mathematics, and How to Avoid Good-Byes

I've been scared of writing this letter since January. It was the day after New Year's, and I'd just ditched dinner to finish a deliciously complex in-house revision when my mom came in and asked how many more times I'd ditch dinner to finish a deliciously complex in-house revision. And I realized, not very many. *Polyphony H.S.* has given me years to study and marvel over the art of pinning thought to paper, but now I find myself tethered to the exhausted expression that I'm at a loss for words. How am I supposed to say what all this has meant?

I wasn't exactly destined to be a poet. My dad is a mathematics professor; my mom does statistical analysis for a living. They met in abstract algebra class in college. As far as familial heritage goes, tinkering with poetry – like falling in love with Debora Greger's "Eve in the Fall" in the ninth grade and spending my spare time lamely trying to reproduce its luminosity – was sort of like heresy. I didn't know it then, but editing for *Polyphony H.S.* was to become the reason my bipolar mind could live with itself, assembling and unraveling both literary and mathematical knots in the same frame of thought. In fact, editing no less than demanded that I do so. Why? Take any good poem, bite into it, and you'll feel the crunch of a matured body torn in two, the crunch of bones. A real poem has no meat, no fat to get in the way. No loose variables in the equation. Only bones, chiseled and whittled and locked together, hinges tight, curves gleaming, angles set into a delicate balance. Enjambing just a hair too late, or mislabeling an apricot as "rosy" instead of "roseate" – that's all it takes to topple a poem. That's all it takes to destroy the logic of a proof. What *Polyphony H.S.* taught me, particularly as an in-house editor, was that the lure of creating an untamed, unbounded line of verse is often more a beguiling trap than a ticket to freedom: every gesture, every slightest swaying of the poet's mind, whether voluntary or not, is stripped naked for the world to see. That demands an almost painful degree of sensitivity on the editor's part. What comforted me as I learned the ropes, though, was the similarity such a mindset held to a mathematician's – probing a proof or solution for the finest leaks in logic, for those flitting moments when the mind chases intuition over rigor and the truth of a theorem evaporates, unnoticed. Things I'd inhaled and exhaled my whole childhood. My calculus teacher once told me that Euler's formula, considered one of the most gorgeous equations in all of mathematics, could draw blood. Over the years that same image became my creed for editing a poem – test your finger against the edge of any line, and it should be keen enough to split skin. It turned out that the deepest instincts of poetry and mathematics were, to my happy surprise, one and the same: to pursue a statement to its purest form, no more and no less. In the end, my years editing at *Polyphony* gave me more than ever promised. They put together my two halves. They reconciled me to myself. That, beyond all else, is what I'm most grateful for.

Clara Fannjiang, *Outgoing co-Editor-in-Chief*

Special shout-out to contributors Cara Dorris (Vol. VI, VII) and Erica Swanson (Vol. VI, VII), who blew my brains apart every time; Audrey Gidman (Vol. VII), who renewed my faith in prose poetry; and Jessica Renfrew (Vol. VI), Jackson Rollings (Vol. VI), Francesca Allegra (Vol. VII), Madeleine Wattenbarger (Vol. VII), Anthony Otten (Vol. VII, VIII), Sera Park (Vol. VIII), and every other author who shamelessly redefined what I believed writing could do and could be.

```
Announcing the Winners of the 2012
Claudia Ann Seaman Awards for Young Writers
```

Poetry Winner

Danny Rothschild, Interlochen Arts Academy, Interlochen, Michigan
for *Under the Light of a Lamppost*

Poetry Judge **Laura Van Prooyen**

Laura Van Prooyen, the author of *Inkblot and Altar* (Pecan Grove Press 2006), has work forthcoming in *The American Poetry Review*, *Boston Review*, and the tenth anniversary anthology: *Best of 32 Poems*. She is a recipient of grants from the American Association of University Women and the Barbara Deming Memorial Fund, and also has been awarded a Dorothy Sargent Rosenberg prize for her creative work. Van Prooyen earned an M.F.A. in Poetry at Warren Wilson College, and she lives in San Antonio. Her second collection of poems, *Resist*, has been a finalist in book competitions and remains under submission.

Literary Nonfiction Winner

Hali Haskins, Woodbridge Senior High School in Woodbridge, Virginia for *3's*

Literary Nonfiction Judge **S.L. Wisenberg**

Sandi Wisenberg is the author of *The Sweetheart Is In* and *Holocaust Girls: History, Memory, & Other Obsessions*, and *The Adventures of Cancer Bitch*. She has an M.F.A. in fiction from the University of Iowa Writers' Workshop and a B.S. from the Medill School of Journalism. She was a feature writer for the *Miami Herald* and has published prose and poetry in *The New Yorker*, *Ploughshares*, *Tikkun*, *New England Review*, *Michigan Quarterly Review* and many other places. She was a blogger for *The Huffington Post* and is the co-director of Northwestern's M.A./M.F.A. in Creative Writing program. She has received a Pushcart Prize and fellowships from the Illinois Arts Council, Fine Arts Work Center in Provincetown and the National Endowment for the Humanities. She was the graduate faculty recipient of the 2006-2007 Distinguished Teaching Award, presented by Northwestern University's School of Continuing Studies.

Fiction Winner

Kate Bell, Claremont Secondary School, Victoria, British Columbia for
My Name is Cassie, and I Will Tell You All You Need to Know about High School

Fiction Judge **Christine Sneed**

Christine Sneed is a graduate of the MFA creative writing program at Indiana University and has published stories in *Best American Short Stories*, *PEN/O. Henry Prize Stories*, *New England Review*, *The Southern Review*, *Ploughshares*, *Pleiades*, *Glimmer Train*, and many other journals. She has been awarded an Illinois Arts Council Fellowship in poetry and received a 2010 Los Angeles Times book prize, first-fiction category, for *Portraits of a Few of the People I've Made Cry*. She lives in Evanston, IL and teaches creative writing and literature courses at DePaul University in Chicago, and creative writing for the University of New Orleans' low residency MFA program.

Congratulations to our winners and thank you to our judges!

The 2013 Claudia Ann Seaman Awards For Young Writers

The Claudia Ann Seaman Awards for Young Writers were created by the Seaman family in memory of their daughter and sister, a young poet. The CAS Awards acknowledge excellence in teen writing in poetry, fiction, and creative nonfiction.

Open to:	All students in grades 9–12
Submission:	Each participant may submit a total of three works: poems, stories, literary nonfiction or any combination. *(1,500 word limit for fiction and literary nonfiction)*
Deadline:	Entries must be received by April 15, 2013
Cash Award:	$200.00 award for each genre
Award Announcement:	Fall 2013
How to Submit:	**Submit your work directly to *Polyphony H.S.*** at www.polyphonyhs.com

- All submissions entered via our online submission process at **www.polyphonyhs.com** are automatically entered into the Claudia Ann Seaman Awards for Young Writers

- Only submissions entered via online submission process at **www.polyphonyhs.com** will be considered for publication

Each entry **must** contain the following information:

- Student name, address, phone number, email address, year of HS graduation
- School name, address, phone number
- Name and email address of student's English or writing teacher

Tony Fitzpatrick

About Our Cover

Orange and Black Bird: Portal to the Mercy of Autumn

Captain James Cook was one of those English explorers who circumnavigated the globe a few times. His interests were largely scientific so he wasn't all bad, as English explorers go. Most of the time they'd land on a new piece of land, declare it the property of the Queen, kill the original inhabitants in the name of Christ and crown and then plunder all of the shit owned by the recently deceased inhabitants. Then, finally, they'd declare the place civilized. They also brought their diseases with them – smallpox, cholera, alcoholism, rickets, scabies and the clap, which they generously spread…

Humans were not the only casualties of the newly introduced smorgasbord of pestilence. The colonists, in every case, also brought house cats to eat rats that infested the ships. And the cats…soon devoured whole populations of birds. The scourge of domestic cats is responsible for the decimation of an IMMENSE number of species of island birds, particularly in Hawaii. Mosquitoes and plume hunters didn't help either, but mostly, it was the domestic cat.

Some months ago I had some fun with bird watchers in my column. I really tweaked the f----s, painting them as a snobby coven of geeks; a cult of 50-year old guys who lived with their moms. I was being an ass as a result of one encounter with a bunch of them in Cape May, New Jersey in which the birdy folk ostracized me for smoking a cigarette outside.

Luckily, a great many of them had a good sense of humor. Two of their number, Joel Greenberg and Greg Neise, have become good friends. Every two weeks I importune these two guys who are naturalists, scientists and life-long birders, and they teach me about birds. I've drawn them since I was a child. They've been a sense of wonder in my life for as long as i can remember. I told these guys about the first time I saw a goldfinch. It was on the ground and just kind of busted to life and flight and nearly touched me in its ascent. I remember running home to my mother and telling her that I'd seen a dandelion turn into a bird.

Both Greg and Joel are endlessly patient with me and the total tonnage of what I don't know. Joel Greenberg devoted 25 years of his life to writing a natural history of Chicago and its environs. He sent the book to me some years ago and it is fascinating. Both he and Greg Neise enlightened me to the frightening decline of jays, blackbirds and crows due to the West Nile virus that ravaged bird populations all over America almost a decade ago. Among birders and naturalists this was a horrifying bell-weather moment, yet also an opportunity to learn something about the mechanics of extinction. Why and how it happens.

One of the best examples of this is Hawaii – a bunch of islands that act almost as kind of a biosphere – in fact, not even kind of. An actual biosphere.

A great many honey creeper family bird species have been wiped out by cats and mosquitoes, much like the Galapagos, another biosphere. Introduced species had the evolutionary advantage over native species in that they could adapt faster to their environment.

The American bluebirds' numbers dropped precipitously when the European starling and the English sparrow were introduced. Both birds were notorious nest thieves. Basically these birds were Joe Pesci with wings. The American bluebird was pushed west of the Mississippi for the most part. Only now, is it beginning to re-establish its range in Illinois, largely through the efforts of birders who carefully monitor the populations of all bird species. Science is aided greatly by the efforts of birders and organizations like the American Birding Association.

So much for my petty jokes about "birdy people." They are part of the solution and I am some dork who draws pictures. They have taught me much and I am grateful for their tolerance and largeness of heart toward dopes like me.

I plan on making a bunch of the extinct and nearly-extinct birds because whether we know it or not, they are part of the magic of our lives, part of the wonder, and in no small way, we share a fate.

....

Tony Fitzpatrick is an artist, poet and actor whose artwork can be found in the collections of the Museum of Modern Art in New York City, the National Museum of American Art in Washington, D.C., the Museum of Contemporary Art in North Miami, the Museum of Contemporary Art in Chicago and the Philadelphia Museum of Art.

Tony has published seven books including three collections of art and poetry: *The Hard Angels* (1988), *Dirty Boulevard* (1998) and *Bum Town* (2001); a collection of etchings entitled *Tony Fitzpatrick: Max and Gaby's Alphabet* (2001) and three collections of drawing-collages entitled, *The Wonder: Portraits of a Remembered City, Volume 1* (2005), *The Wonder: Portraits of a Remembered City, Volume 2, The Dream City* (2006), and *The Wonder: Portraits of a Remembered City, City of Monsters, City of Ghosts* (2008), and *This Train* (2010). His work has also been published in *Poetry*.

Tony Fitzpatrick was born in 1958 in Chicago where he lives today with his wife and two children.

About Us

Polyphony H.S. was founded in August 2004. At that time, there was no other magazine like it in the world; that is, a professional quality, national literary magazine for high school writers, edited by high school students from public, private, and parochial schools; and there is still nothing like it in the world. Not only do our editors invite high school writers to submit their work for professional publication, but they also give editorial feedback to every author who submits a manuscript. This extends to continuing a dialogue with accepted authors in an effort to strengthen each piece.

When we published our first edition in the spring of 2005, we had 156 total submissions. Since then we have received thousands of submissions from students in more than twenty countries, including Australia, Canada, China, Czech Republic, France, German, Hong Kong, India, Kenya, Korea, Latvia, Macedonia, Malaysia, Mexico, Pakistan, Philippines, Puerto Rico, Russia, Singapore, Switzerland, United Arab Emirates, United Kingdom, United States Minor Outlying Islands, and Vietnam.

Originally funded with support from the Latin School of Chicago, *Polyphony H.S.* is now a 501(c)3 non-profit organization, incorporated in the State of Illinois. We are the sole high-school litmag accepted for membership in the Council of Literary Magazines and Presses (CLMP). Published annually, *Polyphony H.S.* accepts submissions from July 1 through April 15.

This year, more than one hundred readers and editors (all high school students) from across the country, read and commented on more than 1400 submissions. Each submission is read and commented on by at least two readers/editors before a final determination is made.

In the summer of 2005 we offered our first National Editor Training (NET) Workshop, inviting high school editors from around the country to join us for an intensive weekend of Editorial Training. These workshops have helped us develop an editorial training method that has prepared more than a hundred editors for editorial positions on university and professional literary magazines. These workshops will be available for students interested not only in editing for *Polyphony H.S.* but for students interested in growing as editors for their own school literary magazines as well. An online workshop has been developed for the 2012-2013 academic year.

Students who are interested in joining our national editorial staff will find applications for our National Editor Training (NET) Workshops in Chicago (summer 2013) and guidelines for First Readers as well. For subscriptions, submissions, advertising, comments, or to find out how you can support us, contact us at www.polyphonyhs.com.

Mission

Our mission is to create a high-quality literary magazine written, edited, and published by high school students. We strive to build respectful, mutually beneficial writer-editor relationships that form a community devoted to improving students' literary skills in the areas of poetry, fiction, and creative non-fiction.

Belief

We believe that when young writers put precise and powerful language to their lives it helps them better understand their value as human beings. We believe the development of that creative voice depends upon close, careful, and compassionate attention. Helping young editors become proficient at providing thoughtful and informed attention to the work of their peers is essential to our mission. We believe this important exchange between young writers and editors provides each with a better understanding of craft, of the writing process, and of the value of putting words to their own lives while preparing them for participation in the broader literary community.

On Mutualism:
The Writer and Editor at Polyphony H.S.

One of the most beautiful phenomena in animal biology is that of mutualism, a form of symbiosis. A mutualistic relationship is one in which two organisms both benefit from their interaction. Such is the editorial process at *Polyphony H.S.* Many mutualistic relationships (like the parable of a bird who flies into a crocodile's mouth to clean its teeth and, in turn, get its food) seem unlikely. And in turn, so might my correspondence with a young writer from Guadalajara. Through the editorial process, authors receive invaluable feedback, while editors like me reap more benefits than I could have ever imagined when I signed up to become a first reader at the beginning of my freshman year.

Hearing the "many voices" (the definition of "polyphony") of our submitting authors makes *Polyphony H.S.* almost addictive to me as an editor. Even though many pieces aren't quite as breathtaking as the ones ultimately compiled in this printed edition, hearing the voices of teenagers is a unique perk to those of us involved with *Polyphony H.S.* Even pieces we don't accept have lines that resonate with me. After spending time with a piece, I find myself with a poignant phrase from that piece echoing in my head. In this strange little symbiosis, our authors have the power to profoundly affect our editors.

But what's really special about reading the pieces is that we all have the same intention in mind: to express ourselves. It wasn't until I read F. Scott Fitzgerald's early short story, *Head and Shoulders*, that I realized how much I actually express myself in my comments to authors, perhaps as much as they express themselves in their pieces. In *Head and Shoulders*, the protagonist, Horace Tarbox – once an aspiring author and child prodigy who now settles for an "unwritten book" while his flapper wife finds success in her colloquially written book – reflects, "Poor gauzy souls trying to express ourselves in something tangible. Trying to choose our mediums and then taking what we get – and being glad."

The only difference between Horace's outlook on expression through something tangible and mine, as an editor, is that we don't just take what we get. The feedback we provide to authors is detailed – perhaps nitpickingly so – but it works toward improvement. Rejected authors often get feedback that's more thorough than the feedback on pieces that ultimately make it to print.

What I've discovered this year is the perfect joy of the in-house editing process, in which we have involved literary correspondences with the authors of pieces that have been accepted for publication. This in-house process allows many of us to have meaningful literary discussions with our peers around the world who are trying to express themselves in tangible ways. We create, with these email correspondences with authors, remarkable, twenty-first century, literary pen-pal relationships. But this is just one of the things that makes being an editor so rewarding.

We develop connections even with our poets and writers whose pieces do not make it to the print issue. Though there may be only seventy-some pieces in this volume, our more than one hundred editors around the country have found something of value in every one of the pieces that have been submitted to us this year.

The nexus is simple at this international magazine for editors and writers; we just get each other. That's what *Polyphony H.S.* is: students around the world who may not know each other, but who understand and care about each other, and who find great value in creative expression.

And we end up with this literary magazine along the way.

Hedy Gutfreund, *rising co-Editor-in-Chief*

Defying Convention: The Character of vol. VIII

Through my three years of working with *Polyphony H.S.*, I have come to learn that each volume has its own personality, its own set of values, its own individual spirit. While some people may attribute these disparate literary identities to the changing population of writers, changing economic patterns, or the evolution of the American teenager – the same "some people" who might typify adolescent fiction as a genre unto itself – I link the individuality of each issue to the growing resolve of *Polyphony H.S.* writers, both new contributors and ol' faithfuls, to create distinct works that increasingly defy literary conventions. This year especially, I have seen writers experiment with new styles, formats, genres, and even reach with courage for the work of literary greats like Gwendolyn Brooks with the induction of the Golden Shovel poem format. *Polyphony H.S.* writers are always trying to push the envelope, always trying to bring nuance and authenticity to each line of their poems and narratives, and distinguish themselves as new voices in the community.

This year, *Polyphony H.S.* has embraced a new format: the Golden Shovel poem. Golden Shovel poems allow the writer to integrate verse from other poems, concluding the last line of the new poem with each word from their chosen poem. This new genre has allowed *Polyphony H.S.* writers to expand their repertoire of composition and rebrand classic works of their literary predecessors with their own voice. It is amazing to me how these writers so deftly pay homage to the respected hall-of-famers while still creating real, original works. Kathleen Cole's "While We Wait for Old Age," a poem about the fragility of life and the universal façade of human invulnerability, derives from Gwendolyn Brooks' poem "Old Mary," a piece about momentary opportunities and the limitations of humanity in the context of time. Both poems make profound, individual statements, yet share a dependence on on imaginative language and creative enjambment, as well as similar thematic undertones of loss. Cole creates a poem that is at once uniquely hers and also a tribute to the legacy of Brooks' lyricism and cutting wit. With Kevin Emery's "American Soft Drink," we are given the same picture of moral relativity as in Brooks' "The Last Quatrain of the Ballad of Emmett Till" – the same spectrum of emotion and color, the same juxtaposition of cynicism and hope. And yet Kevin's poem achieves a oneness that exists independently of the borrowed verse. In the words of fellow editor Rachel Stone, Golden Shovel poems must "assert themselves as independents" in order to be successful. In this light, I think these poems sing.

The evolution of *Polyphony H.S.* writers does not only refer to the community of writers as a whole, but also applies on a much smaller, individual level. *Polyphony H.S.* prides itself on the overwhelming numbers of new writers and editors who join the ranks each year, the people who help the magazine grow and flourish. But the foundation of *Polyphony H.S.* was undoubtedly built by those who have stuck with it for more than one submission, more than one revision, more than one year. Emily Cutler has submitted over twenty pieces from 2009-2012. She has completed multiple revisions, and is one of the most committed contributors *Polyphony H.S.* has seen in its eight year existence. It's people like Emily Cutler who most clearly exemplify the mission of *Polyphony H.S.* editors; she values the process, not just the finished product. With Emily we see the same evolutionary spirit that is present in the trajectory of the magazine. In this year's "Visiting Anna," Emily demonstrates her mastery of character and relationships, her observant nature as both a narrator and a storyteller – skills that were evident in her witty repartee in "Popular Linguistics" and the raw vulnerability of "Six Ways of Hiding" – relics from her earlier *Polyphony H.S.* portfolio. I can only hope that Emily's future literary endeavors were helped by *Polyphony H.S.*'s creative processes, that her submissions not only stand as singular accomplishments, but as lessons in confidence and hard, sometimes painstakingly hard, revision.

Ultimately, this season's issue of *Polyphony H.S.* sheds light on the individual voice and the power to transcend what is familiar. These contributors have given us a diverse body of work that not only illustrates their stories, but adds to our own collective narrative. They give us stories like Phoebe Goldenberg's "Red Cowboy Boots," ringing with honesty and brilliant wordplay ("wisps of money-love"). They give us Peter LaBerge's "Carlisle Blue," a blessing to rhythm, and Madelyne Xiao's "Anachronism," a lesson in subtlety. With each piece we learn as readers, as editors, as human observers.

I want to thank all the editors and contributors that have made this happen for us yet again, and for allowing us to embrace and give stage to their experiments in craft and individualism.

Oly Huzenis, *co-Editor-in-Chief*

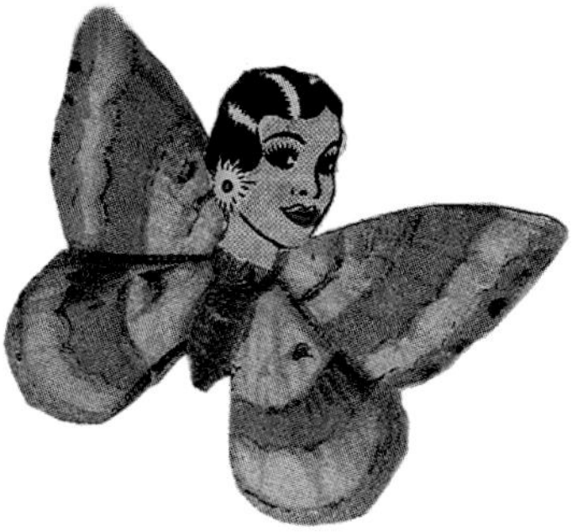

About The Epigraph for vol. VIII

There is a comment field in our online submission program that we reserve for information about our submitting authors' high schools. In keeping with this issue's irreverence for literary convention, we thought we'd share a few of the comments our authors have made over the years that mostly have nothing to do with their high schools.

Reading this always makes me tired.

It's a psychological fear. Enjoy!

This is my first poem i have submitted sorry if it is crappy. It is not my very first poem which is the best i have written (It is lost) :(.

Read it aloud!

This is a risky piece since it concerns sex and how teens deal with it, but rest assured it contains no sex scenes or profanity. It is a tastefully written story.

*I was forced to submit this paper by my teacher,
I would not suggest publishing it.*

I don't actually go to school.

Though at first glance these comments may hint at a compulsion to frivolity on the part of our authors, in my mind the statements more accurately represent one more attempt, by our authors, to reach out to us in some personal way.
We're human beings, they seem to say. *Remember this when you read our work.*
Well – we do remember this when we read your work. As it turns out that's why we exist.

Billy Lombardo
Co-founder/Managing Editor of *Polyphony H.S.*

Clara Fannjiang
Davis Senior High, Davis CA

Bird Under the Lamppost

in the haze of dusk
i watch you,
your quiet games as they
till the soft air

(nothing at your feet
but three pennies
stilled and nameless,
but you scatter them so industriously

into the lamplight –
you, dear bird, who in the art
of your presumptuousness
love nothing better

than that tick and tingle
of light against metal,
that semblance of beautiful
things formed

in little worlds — for isn't that
how you fly, dear bird,
is that not the cleanness
of your buoyancy, maybe nothing

better than faith in pennies
and their lucent morgues,
isn't the void of the sky just that,
a lovely mouth holding you

captive as you now rise
into the dark, vivid and breathless,
like a small girl blowing the husk
of a ladybug back to life)

This is the kind of piece that really excites me. From its deft manipulation of language to its keen understanding of tone to its quiet tension, it's a beautiful read throughout. If this poem doesn't get published, I will be very sad.

Raven Mathewes

Harvard-Westlake School, Los Angeles, CA

Deep Sea Gigantism and a Bioluminescent Utopia

An ocean-woman works her garden with
her fingertips, black rock-heads
crusted with barnacles and sea salt,
dipped into the soil bed with a wooden trowel.
The Earth drops dirt boulders like sugar cubes
into her open water-palms
– a soft plunk and crumble
veiled against the veiny snap of crabgrass.

Yellow-bellied fish swish up from her stomach,
and a blue whale with teeth like a boar-bristle brush
crests up from her womb: indigestion.
Sailors navigate across her collar.
Wire netting twines over her in garlands.

Breathing out the wake of tides,
she reaches down to grab hold
of roots to bury.
This is her rejection of folklore:
quietly pressing around a white hemlock bulb
beneath wilted banana peels and deep breaths.

This piece subtly captures the rhythm and spirit of the ocean in all of its beauty, struggle, and, most of all, charm. The charm is understated but ingenious. The more I read it, the more I obsess over it.

Rocío Guenther

The American School Foundation of Guadalajara, Jalisco, Mexico

Coconuts

Flies swarm around the coconuts' open cocoons, hoping for a taste of juice. But he doesn't let them get it. Pedro shoos them away – he doesn't let them have a taste of that freshness. People gather. They cluster around his cheap whitewashed plastic table. "Cocos frescos," he bellows, puncturing straws into the opening green layers that rim the inside of the white fruit. Pedro's scruffy beard heightens with his playful smiles as he beams at his buyers. His humid tank top sticks to his cinnamon brown skin like glue. He smells of salt and sweat. Chopping coconuts brings pleasure, gives freshness from a hot day at the beach to his rambling customers. Coconuts are hard – hard enough to break someone's head. But coconuts quench thirst. Coconuts help the marooned and the shipwrecked survive in desert islands. Coconuts help Pedro provide.

During breaks, Pedro pushes through the rumbling waves, immerses himself into salty splashes. Las olas, the waves: his favorite place to be. As he walks near the shore, the sun starts to hide behind the horizon. The waves unwind and retreat, and the sand soaks up the salty residue. The sun dips under. Foam bubbles away between his toes. His body claps against the wind, and he closes his eyes.

***

Night brings forth the stars – silver thorns decorating the black atmosphere. They give him comfort. Underline his dreams. Pedro walks on the cobblestone road in his raunchy town of Lo de Marcos. Bungalows, trailer parks, bilingual menus provided in restaurants. The beach is consistently filled with passersby who get excited by cheap beach tattoos and braids with colorful beads. For Pedro, it means more coconuts are sold. Pedro trudges through the dunes, leaving the shops and taco stands behind; he hears breaths of pleasure by the moonlight. Standing behind a palm tree he sees lovers coiling in the sand, wrapped in a turquoise blanket. The stranger grabs the woman's long black hair, and curls it in his fingers. Pedro leaves. It's not his place to be anymore. Pain simmers inside of him as he remembers.

Stolen kisses under the moonlight. Late night dippings into the ocean. Shared coconuts on slippery black rocks. Whispered secrets with Her beneath the stars. Running back to his stand, he gathers a few coconuts, brings them to the beach. Tears hang on his lower lids, as he throws a coconut into a sharp-pointed rock. Juice spilling. Tears spilling. In the middle of the night when the breeze blows palm tree leaves to the sand, and when the stars shine brightest, you can hear Pedro and his coconuts, cracking.

✹

The idea of Pedro and his coconuts cracking extends far beyond this story. The piece acts as a chilling yet succinct exposé into a faltering human soul, perhaps reflecting on the human need for catharsis. Simply wonderful.

Emma Arett

Metro Academic and Classical High School, St. Louis, MO

Lady Sing the Bruise

1
at fourteen, i left home
for new mexico

    (have suitcase, will write)

to camp – with big dreams
and a round face

i searched for love, but found fragments of sappho
among the knots and brambles in my unwashed hair

i was baptized by fire
and sent, still smoldering,
into the dry hot arms of my blessed savior:

"skinny colorado"

who wrote his eternal pastiche on napkins, hashing things out,
hopped up and propelled by the evergreenest weed

    (mind buzzing faster than pen could move against paper)

and contemplating his sweet, sweaty nightmare desire
to become a howling hero –

the desire to be anything to be more than that slight, slithering
night creature whose tongue fit perfectly
into my great gorge,

who stole quarters from the laundry
and sprouted wings after midnight
to fly,

wiry and free like a kite against the titanic sky

Emma Arett

2
you are holy, you are holy, you are holy

but unsure – you hesitate,
delicate as bone and ink,
quietly ignoring

how the lallation, a betrayal by your tongue to your brain,
seizes and jerks in the space between us like a fledgling spider,

from then on we communicate in mandarin
    (ni hao ni hao ni hao)
and the universal language of fingertips –

a hodgepodge of my heritage
and yours: mixed and unrecognizable
like the wooly knots in your hair in the morning

this is the dreamy second love
waking up sleepy and entangled
the dreamy, drizzly second love

forged from skin
and more-than-skin:

haunting, flesh, hope

that you have found a home
somewhere here, between guizhou and heaven.

*

A perfect balance between showing and telling. There's a lot of mystery in this piece; it's a poem that asks you to read it and reread and read again. It shifts from the personal into a love story. It's subtle, ephemeral, and self-assured.

Madelyne Xiao
Urbana High School, Ijamsville, MD

Anachronism

averse to the ebb and flow of time,
my grandfather
(shriveled husk of a man)
dons the regalia of his youth
in the light of liminal dawn to march
the pace of another morning
away from inevitable
colophon.

It's a skillful, quick, keen, discerning, full-fleshed portrait of a man in just eight lines. The title relates to the last line, which is in itself an anachronism that must be understood in its old meaning to be sensible, but then closes the poem brilliantly. An instant in time, explored, illuminated. This poem shines.

Retreat, 2007

Margaret Sullivan
York Suburban High School, York, PA

The dog has been running all day on the mesa and soon it will die. For now, you have left the leash back at the house that you rented for the retreat. It is a house built deep in the Sonoran Desert, no service or septic and, after sunset, no light. You like the sound of that name, Sonoran. All four paintless walls are scoured like bone and the windows gape empty-mouthed over sills with fake begonias and fake Navajo pottery.

There is so little rain here in this valley that it is named after Death. But on this day it has rained.

Your old dog has been catching the raindrops on the green flatlands with its teeth. It shakes its head and growls as if ripping the water from the air. You can see through the windows that the dog is returning, the yellow half-moon behind it along the dirt road to your retreat house.

You have done well here, finished three paintings and prepared the sketches for two more; in a few weeks, you will pack up and return to Seattle. Only artists, you think, can have a victorious retreat.

The dog is strictly not allowed in the rented house, but it's not as if anyone is going to drive out here to check. In the Greyhound Bus, you sat in the far back next to an overweight casino lord and fed the dog kibble on the sly. You have been through a lot in the past few years, this dog and you, and you talked to it during the ride, shared inside jokes:

"Do you remember when I had to hide you in the clothes hamper from the landlord? You were so quiet and good. You're glad that's over, aren't you? Aren't you, boy? It's all better now. Yes, good boy."

More of the nubbly beef-colored kibble fed through the bars. More lonely conversations with the dog than you would like to admit. It's a Golden Retriever, a rescued dog, its fur not golden now but shackled with mud from the mesa and its sides heaving like undersea vents as it lays down before you on the carpet, shivering. You kneel.

The dog's breath is humid when you put your hand down around its muzzle. There is a soft rhythm to it. There's my good boy. The dog does not look up at you but rather past you, toward the green mesa and the rain plummeting like stained glass toward the earth. It whines. No, not long now.

You think that there was one other night that was just like this. You are wrong, of course, but memory is as close as the blue paint on your hands, and it smells of turpentine.

There was a class in college led by a visiting professor whose name escapes you, doesn't matter now. It was late to still be in the studio but you and four other students had stayed behind to finish sketching a project. This transient professor wandered back and forth behind you in tiny dark-green heels that matched her dust-colored clothing. She walked in a small rhythm under rows and rows of florescent lights.

This professor who stayed only for that semester began to recite a poem for you and the four other students who stood there sketching. Biblical gusts of rain were falling and the sound of it filled the room along with her voice. The professor's recitation grew louder and louder but you did not look behind you, did not see her face. You drew another grim charcoal line on the creamy skin of the paper and then another, not seeing. She had eight months to live. You did not see her shaping the words that lifted you through hellfires of blood-eyed pigeons, rages, flames melting the sky-colored frosting off birthday cakes, troops of twisted metal and unending Mobius loops that emerge as a photographic negative, black eyes with wormhole-white centers.

It is just as she intended. The five sketches assembled there will be the best any of you have ever made. You will never understand it precisely this way again, those sounds converging. You with your back still to this terminally ill professor and so you never saw her face at the moment she began to weep. To break. To realize.

Her expression was hidden to you all these years but how it comes to you now. It slips into your mind's blank, white eye as you sit holding your dog in a house of chosen isolation. Good boy, good boy, you say.

You will live through many other rain-softened nights and re-enter many other houses. That much is certain. But in your mind's eye, you will still be here, kneeling on the coarse orange carpet in Death's valley. The memory is gone now but you hear a voice speaking that must be yours. Or perhaps it is the professor's. The dog's breath retreats. The expression on the professor's face. Was it wonder or despair? You must decide now, which. Just as there is no escape from the voice speaking with slow, steady tones, asserting what you already know. What you have now, you cannot have or create again. Never. Not in any other way but this.

✻

> *There's an exquisite balance here between clarity and what could be called, I suppose, "literariness" – it's plainly written but not simplistic, neither obvious nor abstruse. It's the kind of writing that makes me want to keep to myself a bit in search of my own retreat.*

Anjie Liu

New Hartford Senior High School, New Hartford, NY

Jackson Pollock

I wonder
if even Jackson Pollock couldn't tell apart
his own paintings from say

if I ran around
on the same type of
canvas he used
with little buckets of the same
shades he used
and spewed them the same
way he did
if I did a really good job of that

I thought I found you
at a sushi bar in the airport
but he was empty like a thirsty man caught
between the Indian and the Pacific

it's like the wall with holes
different women sticking out faceless hands
for the poor child to identify
the mother

which is why
I always feel guilty when
for a second
I mistake short black-haired women
at the grocery store
for my mom
because it shouldn't happen

and maybe I'm biased
because his lips didn't tremor
a 4.3 on the Richter Scale
like yours did
when your boy left
and he didn't kiss that boy goodnight
with an embarrassed flicker of the eyelash
like you did
when your boy left

I forgot what came out of the wall of hands
it's somewhere
but I don't want to find it

besides, Pollock is dead
which is why I could never
hike up the stairs two steps at a time
to his old New York apartment
with his real No. 5 and my fake
and demand that
he choose the right one
and maybe see that faint disconcerted glimmer
for a second
behind the folds of his eye wrinkles
maybe

Anjie Liu

but why Jackson Pollock
what was he even
I'd rather ask
you
if you would know
my bitten fingernails
my handwriting
my hairline maybe
from all the others
only I'd rather you not answer
only you are struggling
to discern that boy's voice
from the cacophony of your fate

just like when after that reckless beverage truck
my sister lost my name somewhere on the highway
and in the soft patterns of hospital gowns

why, I don't even have a sister
and I feel this way.

✻

As a bit of a Jackson Pollock fan, I was initially skeptical but this piece won me over. It uses this hypothetical Pollock impersonation metaphor as a vehicle to discuss something bigger. The imagery is great, the poem itself is not too concrete or too abstract, and it has an extremely powerful ending.

Lilian Kong

Wheeler School, Providence, RI

Amerika

Midnight is
layered liberally
in the stubborn curls of my
violently straightened bangs,
under which lie two dark gesshoku[1]
floating above
fragrant desert of dried mokuren petals that
bleed pink to hide ivory secrets.
The granular Osakan sands of my skin,
explosively dormant,
noxious with the marriage
of Neutrogena
and pressed lychee juice.
And I look at my reflection
trying to block out
your poisonous prayers that
my perpendicular
accent will dissolve into
flatness, and thin out
into lethal white diamond.
You and your snake tongue –
ignoring tear-streaked whispers
from my cherry blossom lashes,
the pleading lines on my forehead
before you every morning as you,
with your thickest foundation
and reddest lipstick,
tell me I must learn
how to live properly in
Amerika, kimu medaru no tochi –
America, the land of gold.

I feel like I've made a friend in the narrator by the time I'm finished reading the piece. Whether you're black or Jewish or Romanian or Peruvian – no matter what your heritage – we've all felt pressure to fit into the "American" mold. While this piece deals with it through a Japanese perspective, it's refreshingly universal.

[1] *Japanese Romanization for 'lunar eclipse'*

Lylla Younes

Louisiana School for Math, Science, and the Arts, Natchitoches, LA

Billy

When you tell me stories,
I watch

as thin strips
of film
wrap around
your eyes,

playing memories
like your
radio played
Bobby Darin
in '65.

And your soul is
a snapshot,

an old polaroid
stashed
in a box with

yellowing baseball cards
and broken plastic toys.

When I'm gone,
you say,

You can find me there.

Lylla Younes

In that dusty box
of forgotten dreams –

Of remnants
worn around the seams –

a skinny boy
in ripped blue jeans –

And wrinkles creased.

And your mouth
        hangs
                slightly
                        ajar.

I have never seen an old man weep.

So underplayed – like a pale leaf slipping from an unseen tree, that even if you were to just sneeze while reading it you might miss its beauty. If you can keep the sneezes in the whole way through, though, it's a lovely fingerprint of the memory of this man, spun from memories and emotions so fleeting you almost feel like they're gone by the last line.

Stephanie Guo
Canyon Crest Academy, San Diego, CA

Cecilia had a Brightness

after Gottfried Benn, translated by Michael Hofmann

Cecilia had a brightness, a shimmer swallows
mistook for the sun. They'd flutter near, sip
the dew from nearby bushes, speed
away when she returned to the loft. And
then Edison – no – Tesla, invented electricity. Suns, all night.

*(Fun fact: "Cecilia" means "way for the blind" in Latin.
The three syllables also make for a really fun drawl.)*

�֍

This is quirky and bright (pun intended) and, dare I say, illuminating. It's as if it fills in the missing pieces in the borrowed line. A lovely read.

Fridays in the Speakeasy

after Gwendolyn Brooks

Clutch that laundry change tight and
Go on, claim they're Spanish pieces of eight, strut
That linty moolah all the way down
Mulberry Street. Taste that lie, savor it. This is the
Place pigeons wing away, streets
Where you couldn't catch them with
Your bare hands if you wanted to. Paint
Those eyes with borrowed serendipity all the way down
To that rented Rolls-Royce; you and your
Fridays in the speakeasy. About face.

This poem has a certain sassy quality to it, like it's snapping its fingers at you and saying something like, "GURL! No you di-n't."

The Offering

you were pale, spurting too many feet
when you touched down
on trembling grass.

i asked, what is your name
and you said it is naïve,
what is yours, i said
i am too old
for introductions. besides,
you know it already.

i invite you into the house.
your gaze wanders the pabulum halls
as you take the first steps in. I ask
why you are here.

you drink tea from a cup
lukewarm between your palms
pinky sticking out
like a peeping mouse

and you tell me,
i have come
to see if young love
is as expensive
as at the department store.

find me
a boy, any XY
Z, I ain't picky.

i want
to see if it hurts, if
picking the scab
is like gazing upon
the feverish artist in the coffee shop:
you want to give him your extra biscuit
but it's too romantic, that
isn't the point. here
there is a flower arrangement of poesies
you can't put your finger on.

i tell you to come back
when you know the difference
between Pepsi and Coke.*

you tell me my
biscuit is stale.

*"the difference between Pepsi and Coke"
  is borrowed from David Lehmann.

This poem is memorable; it's understated. The figurative language and wordplay are beautiful. Great attention to craft, especially in its use of enjambment as stylistic manipulation.

John Richards

Oakwood School, North Hollywood, CA

Red Line

1.

I tried to avoid standing but that wasn't an option.

The subway was packed. Really, I'd never seen anything like this before. Who rides the subway? This was supposed to be my little way of being alone for an hour.

I'm assuming she was his mother. She looked weathered. Like someone had left her strung up on the eaves of a gas station in New Mexico. Once they came back out to take her down, the effects of the sun, wind, and sand had been a little too rough. So they put her in a tight, rhinestone-covered shirt and confined her to a steel tube under the earth.

He was…I'm not sure. A face lost in a crowd. Any man in his twenties you could pass by every day. One five hundredth of a five hundred man march.

I was standing nearby. A prime stand. He had his head on her right shoulder and was asleep. Or pretending to be. She had her right index finger in her mouth. Her left hand was tightly clutching a plastic market bag. Thank you for shopping here. Thank you for your time. Thank you for your money. Thank you.

She pulled her finger out of her mouth. A trail of saliva and the layer on her finger shone a little bit. A star. She wiped her finger off in his hair. Somehow, he didn't notice. The finger returned to its oral case. Her eyes closed, the finger exited once more. She wiped it off in his hair. One last time she repeated the action. She looked around. Had someone caught her in the midst of her ritual?

She closed her eyes for a few moments and turned towards him. She licked his hair. A mother cat. She licked again. And then to his forehead, and again his hair. Three licks, she was done. She fell asleep. What had I seen?

2.

The train had been delayed. I was standing on the platform with roughly twenty other people, waiting. More were coming down the escalator. A group of kids, and then, walking calmly but with intent, the most terrifying man I'd ever seen. I don't know what it was, but this man struck in me an unimaginable fear. The kind of fear that doesn't only swallow you whole, but keeps you in an intestinal pouch. It then waits a while before regurgitating you. A second round to chew its cud. Another few moments as you sit in its mouth, part of a paste of you. A you paste. A sticky sweet glob. The kind of fear that leaves you like a stack of paper. A breeze and your top fifteen sheets are blown off. Each slight gust taking away a sliver of your existence, leaving you with nothing but the memory of a chill as a page slides off your top.

Yet somehow here I was still existing, goosebumps rising on my skin as I was unable to look away from this man still approaching. What was it about him? He had long hair, down to his waist almost. And a beard that reached just a couple of centimeters past his clavicles. His face was flat, his eyes protruded slightly. He was an insect. A hairy, subterranean terror-bug. Yet it wasn't really his face so much as the air he brought with him. It was just something nauseous you could feel from the prickling of your skin as he stood only yards away, his long hair brushing past his arms. He didn't exude rage; there was no bloodlust. Just a sickening feeling pervading the air around him, that air making its way toward me. I had to back up and steady myself against a pylon for fear of collapsing. And I knew exactly what he wanted to do. He was going to charge me from behind and shove me onto the tracks. He wouldn't have to kill me himself. The train would do it. I knew that was what he was going to do. I knew that was what he wanted to do. So I got on the train that had just arrived, even though it wasn't the one I'd been waiting for. It wasn't an accident. I just had to get away. If I had stayed, well, there would have been bits of me all over the tracks. I knew that was what he wanted to do. I knew that was what he was going to do. He was going to rush up behind me and throw me onto the tracks. I can see his stance as he does it. Stay low, the low man wins the war. He must have had some training in football. How else would he have known? Bend the knees, charge with an upward, sweeping motion.

✱

There's an exquisite manipulation of imagery in shaping entire microcosms of life and emotion. The savoring flavor of the narration creates a perspective that is wholesome and so wonderfully human. There is no bravado or mighty, strenuous revelation snuck in here, but I admire the patient, barefaced lyricism to life.

Anna Blech
Hunter College High School, New York City, NY

Sonnet in a Stuffy Room

There is no fate this grueling that I know.
Behind my hair, my eyes are foggy glass.
Fluorescent lights too bright, my mind too slow
Thus do I bear my curse in science class.

My teacher's accent wafts across the room,
Its soporific cadence low and deep.
Behind my lids, tonight's assignments loom,
So many notes to take before I sleep.

Oh deities and angels, listen well!
You patron gods of academic strife,
Don't leave my pleas unanswered; hear my yell!
And I will tell you what I want from life:

To live as free as dancing winds of June,
And each and every day to sleep 'til noon.

This poem manages not to drown under the weight of its rhyme scheme, instead using it as an excuse to not take itself too seriously. It's clever, and funny, and every student on the planet will nod at this and say "that's so true."

Rachel Stone

Latin School of Chicago, Chicago, IL

Twenty-Four

I want you in fistfuls,
to tear up topsoil and excavate abdominals and silence and

sun-burnt sand; waist-deep in
summer-rust and sarcophagi,

even with your German ex-girlfriend's last name of
edelweiss-and-brown-breaded
lilt.

I want you for a mayfly minute, before
the stained-glass shatters and all is left in thread and
dusk.

Every word in this poem was chosen so deliberately. From the title and the "mayfly minute" that allude to the twenty-four hour lifespan of a mayfly to the deft depiction of desire in "I want you in fistfuls," this poem is a special one.

Firefly

I stole my first second when I was seven.

I was alone and almost airborne, shade-mottled shins dangling off Wrightwood Park's tallest tree, perched at the nexus where branch becomes twig. I dropped ribbons of August leaves and watched as stroller tracks wove parallels like a street map, carving arteries and palm lines. I could even see the rust on the swing-set's hinge.

So I stole it.

And all the way home I held the little glass jar with my moment in it, 4:17 sunlight throwing shadows on my car seat when I peeked it out of my pocket like a firefly. Catching it was like a firefly too.

By the time I was twenty-four, my shelves were heavy with jars. Most of them were blue at this point, blue like dusk and the promise of an evening. But some were other colors, too. Two ticks before twelve was eyelash-black. Graduation was orange, Tropicana-bright and full of fructose. An arabesque, soft and resting on quarter notes, was a nice blush tone.

The seconds we spent unpacking your suitcases, when you agreed to share toothbrushes and I thought I loved you was lemon-bright and possible.

Stirring salt into my water glass was porcelain white, selfish and suspended.

It was March and you were running your fingertips across eggshell paint, scratching at the grout and searching for seconds. Were they marigolds, the flowers on my windowsill? You sounded so helpless. I smashed the jar by your antibacterial soap and wove the second hands into your hair. They were Delphinium. I remember Delphinium.

You asked what the jars were for, and I said insurance. I still keep all of your seconds by my alarm clock, an amber uncorked.

The idea is original and luminous; it reminds me of a Kevin Brockmeier story. I love that this piece is, for all its symbolism, surprisingly subtle and delicate.

Deborah Malamud
Harvard-Westlake School in Los Angeles, CA.

A Dead Shirt

I wore a dead person's shirt.
I was young, but not oblivious
and I didn't believe in ghosts.
So there was no last time,
no last word.
I wore her.
And my mother, not only unflinchingly but as though there was
  no reason to shudder told
me to wear it in good health.

I spent some time inventing memories
after the funeral
I didn't go to.
And I thought death a boat shipwrecked. Because it must
  have purpose –
one which, unless searched for,
is not found.

And I spent a lot of time breaking my own heart.
I curled into the arm of my One Month Stranger,
half hallucinating,
and mused to him that there are only two things one can be.
Three, he said. Alive, dead, and in love.
It rang in my ears as he didn't kiss me.
I soaked my tears in a dead person's shirt
and then I lost it,
and death's a boat.

I love the narrator's voice. It's brittle, forthright, and terrifically tangible. Through the simple symbol of a shirt, this poem conveys haunting images and phrases, like that there are three things one can be, "Alive, dead, and in love."

Dylan Combs
Fine Arts Center, Greenville, SC

Aurals

after Basho

Waves of heat penetrate the earth; it's
summer of summer; stupor, never quiet.
Impossible to single out any one noise from them all –
my left ear can contain no more, no less, than the right.
The frogs' croaks attempt to devour crickets' chirps, and the
wind wishes to howl louder than the dog and his cries.
Somehow, though, I can't forget the resonant screech of
shells clung to bark, the discarded layers of chitin, the
vessels that once produced sound now shed by unseen cicadas.
Momentary deafness popped my ears, as, over the sink,
I scrubbed the oils off my face and blew my nose into
the lukewarm torrents of chlorinated tap water, the
drain, the dank silence that saturates subterranean rocks.

This piece captures the essence of Basho's haiku with a quiet grace that reminds me of a hot, still summer night. The imagery is breathtaking. It amazes me that a poem so focused on sound could create such overwhelming visual images as well.

Emily Cutler

Indian Springs School, Birmingham, AL

Visiting Anna

California Pizza Kitchen doesn't just smell like their famous barbecued chicken pizza. It also smells like fresh dough and sweat. Marvin sets up the silverware in his daughter's place while he is waiting for her, taking careful time to line up the knife and spoon. He straightens his back and tries to relax his fingers to look at his watch, then at the door. He can feel the rigid bones in his neck. They do not relax when his daughter Anna walks through the door.

Marvin marches to the door to meet her, forcing his feet to move forward. Her lower lip protrudes the same way it always has, and the groove under her nose has the same narrow width, something Anna inherited from her mother. Marvin's eyes settle on her hair, unwavering from its dull gold color, like sand under the shade of a willow tree. But he notices that her locks have grown an extra inch, and the slight difference makes his chest tighten and his throat harden.

"Anna," he says, and Marvin does not hug her, but instead he grasps her, so much so that his nails almost dig into her skin.

Anna laughs. "Dad." She steps out of his arms and kisses him on the cheek in the spot she always does. Although she cannot see, she has kissed him in that spot, just below his cheekbone, since she was a little girl. Marvin halfway smiles. He places his palm between her shoulder blades and tries to keep his fingers from trembling as he guides her toward the table.

"You should've let me pick you up from campus," Marvin says. He presses his palm more firmly into her back so that he can feel her ribs against the bottoms of his fingers. "It would've been no problem."

"It's really fine. My friend Kate is going to a concert right around here, so she had no trouble taking me. Riding with her was fun." Her voice sounds the same. She speaks with the perfect balance of a soprano pitch and keen fullness that has always reminded Marvin of peaches.

"You had a safe trip?"

"Sure, Dad. It was no big deal."

He helps Anna into the chair and shows her where he has placed the silverware. "You need to be careful. I don't know this girl, and you can't see if she was texting while driving, or paid too much attention to the radio. I want you to be careful about who you drive with." Anna nods. When Marvin sits down he stares at Anna's sand-colored hair and tries not to notice the added length. "This is Anna," he thinks. And he knows she is Anna, because her voice still reminds him of peaches and her eyebrows are still that beautiful silver shade that both offsets and complements her yellow hair.

But at the same time the girl in front of him is not Anna. If this were Anna she would have come home to him every afternoon for the past six months. She would have asked him to drive her to California Pizza Kitchen and to guide her to the front door of the restaurant. Her hair would be an inch shorter, and she would be the little girl clinging to his leg, not the woman who had decided to attend college six thousand miles away from home.

He wonders what to say. He wants to ask her if she is finished with her homework for tonight and if anything interesting happened at school today. He wants to go through each class in order and ask what she learned in each one, and he wants to ask how each of her friends is. But these are not the questions Marvin has asked for the past three months that Anna has been in college, and these are questions he will never ask again. Anna takes Marvin's usual role as the conversation starter and asks the first question. "Did you have a nice flight over?"

"Yes, it was nice. A good flight. They served those sweet Biscotti cookies you like."

"Lucky! You should've saved me some!" Anna smiles with all of her teeth. Marvin is still amazed that her teeth are whiter than her skin.

Marvin bows his head and stares at the wooden table in front of him. "I'm so sorry," he says. "I forgot. I remembered at first…and then, I don't know what came over me. I'm so sorry. I always remember."

"Dad, I was joking. It's okay. Relax."

He doesn't raise his head. He bites the inside of his mouth and buries his face in the menu. He tries to distract himself by looking at the different prices, but every time he remembers the cookies his stomach crinkles.

Finally, Anna says, "Did you get to see much of Iowa City?"

Marvin shakes his head. "I just concentrated on getting to the restaurant. I wanted to get here on time."

"Really?" Anna's eyes bulge. She may not be able to see out of them, but her eyes might be her most expressive feature. "Well you have to see it. Iowa City's not the biggest, but everything is so unique. Once you leave campus, you walk down just two blocks, and you'll find the best coffee shop – it's even better than Starbucks. They have the best chocolate croissants. Then, right across from there is the pie milkshake place – oh, I forget the name already – but you won't find anywhere else with such rich milkshakes. Then to the right of that restaurant is the best used bookshop in the whole world. Actually, their braille section is just so-so, but sometimes I shop there just for the smell – this scent of ink and clean new pages, but it also smells like…history, you know? Oh, I just absolutely have to show you tomorrow."

Anna continues like this. Her eyes move as she describes the city, her pupils dilating over her silver blue iris. She guides Marvin through the city so that in his mind he can taste the milkshakes and smell the bookshop. Without having seen the city he knows what he will see when she shows him tomorrow.

Marvin remembers showing Anna her neighborhood when she was tiny. He remembers trying to describe the colors of the houses and the shape of the mailboxes, guiding her small fingers across the texture of the brick and walking through the shape of a cul de sac. He remembers holding her hand and showing her where to go if she were to ever get lost. Anna depended on him.

"Dad," she says, suddenly stopping in the middle of her description, "I'm so glad you're here."

Marvin's fingers soften and his back relaxes. He eyes wander toward the ends of Anna's hair and he admires the new length. Somehow it makes her look taller. A waiter comes to take their order, and Marvin is not surprised when Anna orders something different than her usual.

After the waiter leaves Anna talks more. She talks about being about her foreign language major, about how the different languages create sounds with different personalities, different textures, how she can see them. "For the first time in my life," she says, "I found something I'll be able to know."

Marvin says, "You always did have a gift for understanding." He is no longer her protector. Anna no longer depends on him. She has her own city and her own world that he is not part of. But Marvin knows he will learn to be happy for her.

Marvin leans forward. He reaches his arm across the table and places his hand on top of Anna's, the top of his palm against her small fingers. "Anna," he says. She clasps his hand in return.

"Your mother would be so proud."

For a moment there is silence. The atmosphere is still. Marvin closes his eyes and focuses on Anna's small hand clasped in his. He feels her thin, bony fingers and soft palms, fragile but strong. He wonders if this is how Anna sees.

Marvin opens his eyes. He looks at Anna, and he sees her. And he smiles.

*

There are no car chases or life-shattering revelations here – this story works in its own way, on its own time. It's very real-seeming; it grows on you, and the ending is quietly gorgeous. cleanly written and self-contained.

Jonah Haven
Walnut Hill School for the Arts, Natick, MA

Belonging

Even with inhibitions clear,
such waves as these constantly
break against me
as birds break form against
the wind – shifting still,
black kites above.

Their waning wings become almost
Indiscernible, like a scar healing;
we run apart and allow
erratic trees to engulf them.
Watching less chastely
than mild men, the wind takes us
to lesions in Earth, one by one.

Until nothing becomes none.
And the birds have forgotten
the wind that ailed them, the sand
that calmly diminished them;
death in darkness floods and we resume,
then resist! in flame, in light,
saturating all,
elating doubt.

*

It reads like a Sylvia Plath poem: the ebb and flow of "resume, then resist!", the complementary contradiction in "such waves! ... break against me / as birds break form," the beauty in "their waning wings become almost / indiscernible like a scar healing," and before we know it, the poem has whisked us through to its orgastic conclusion, the "flame, in light," under which we can remove any remaining doubt that there's something indelibly fantastic at work here.

The Silence that Breathing Takes
(for my father)

In that shallow silence that all breathing takes,
Forget drowning seeds that once grew:
The wild birds of your son's adolescence
That flew North instead of South,
Hearing nothing   at all

From you. Where does this stand?
The fringes of passion, of rage, for which we wait,
Come without notice. They continue our lives'
Tender fires. The ashes tempestuously expect
Sounds geese make yanked down from the surface.

A snapping turtle will understand
These moments' skins, how they assure his pulpy center,
The seeds within the pit: another room hidden from life
And its grit. Leave these moments behind; rip the peel, crack the core,
Drop the bitter seeds – a mouse will eat them.

✻

Oof, this poem is beautiful. It's got a muscle and meat to it that brings me to my knees. I would cross rivers for this poem.

Peter LaBerge
Greens Farms Academy, Westport, CT

Carlisle Blue

Date: September 8, 1992
6:15 p.m.

Missus Emily glowers, waving the dishcloth back and forth in front of my eyes. "Why don't you listen to me?"

"I don't know," I say. A counterfeit smile warms my lips.

"Well, get it together. I didn't have to take you in, girl. If you aren't going to pull your weight around here, then back out you can go."

"I'll help. I promise now," I say. She turns on her heels and rattles away like a huffing express train, and I'm already back thinking, I don't need that woman anyways, (and some more) by the time she rumbles through the door.

~

I don't need that woman anyways. I'm strong. And you, Carlisle, you're strong too. You've seen syringes cause blood to strike our father's eyes until, like naked fish, he started to stink. You saw the bruises that became of it. When you were little, Carlisle, he told you it was the stink that purpled Mama's skin and you, Carlisle, you believed him.

~

And yet the curtains in my room are dipping their toes farther and farther into the outside air. The beginning of September has already brought with it a nagging chill – isn't that strange? I never remember it getting this cold when you were here until November, December even. Did you take the warmth with you? I wouldn't be surprised if it were there with you right now, locked up tight in your suitcase and stroking the inner lining.

Perhaps I really should be going downstairs now. Maybe the Missus means it this time. The only thing worse than a biting draft from those playful curtains and a woman who cares enough to flap her dishcloth in my face with legitimate exasperation is having neither one.

But I really do feel I must unpack my emotions, one folded thought at a time. It's dangerous, I know. Believe me, the Missus has told me plenty of times. You know how she gets when I think about the past. Goes on and on about how greedy it is, how it tends to acquire a uniquely parasitic nature. How I should spend time on worthwhile things like knitting, or cooking, or reading, or bathing, so I don't stink like naked fish.

~

We believed everything he said. Everything, Carlisle, you believed until Mama sagged against the dripping-red mattress beaten like an out of season Georgia Pride peach. And even then I still believed him. But you saw our father's molded fist by the doorway, and then you knew.

Truth is a funny thing, Carlisle, and then you wanted none of it. So you told yourself not to see, and you didn't. You waited, curled like an unborn fetus hidden behind the staircase. Carlisle, you waited and felt our father click the door shut, Mama rub her skin free of red. You waited as you heard the whisper of Mama's blotchy nightgown as it hit the floor with a defeated swish, and the washing machine stumble into its rhythmic drowning of the night's events. You felt the origins of morning sun prick your neck as it taunted the still-dark world. And that's when our father told you, "She's blue 'gain now," and you told him you knew.

Carlisle, you knew, and nobody else – not even me – why she blued during the nights and cried during the days. You knew all of it, everything you needed to know. Especially why. So you told him you knew why she was bluing like the underbelly of a marlin. And Carlisle, that's another funny thing: why. You told him it was a funny thing, but he didn't agree. Then you got blue. A funny thing.

And all the while, I never understood you. I still don't – perhaps that's why I feel obligated, encouraged to write all of this down, and achieve a sort of conclusion to clear my head and expel the condition Missus Emily says I have.

I don't know whether she has found out about the blue still feasting like maggots on my skin – how permanent and loyal it remains clinging to the surface, holding within it everything we stood for.

~

Lids lifted to take a breath from the surface, I see the Missus standing at my door, speechless.

"What's the matter?" I ask her casually.

"Get yourself up and go eat. The Lord knows you need it."

There's more she wants to say – I can tell – but she buries whatever it is under her tongue and turns quickly on her heels.

8:36 p.m.

I still don't need that woman. Now that I think of it, I also don't need this hellacious shade of blue. It's sitting stubbornly on my thigh right now refusing to evaporate from underneath my skin, and I can't help but wonder whether you could dissipate it if you were here.

Something I do need is a little truth. Carlisle, without it I don't know how much longer I'll be in this room, with the curtains walking out into the September air. I don't know how things will go back to normal – your sleeping body next to mine under the blanket conveniently in the keeping room next to where our father slept. Like corn in the pantry, our bodies were stored, ready for shucking.

Until the night the tempestuous wind beat the melody out of the chimes on the porch. That night, when our father crept into our room, thinking us asleep, you showed him what we really were. You showed him, Carlisle, not I, that we were more than two ears of butter-and-sugar yellow. We were powerful. The two of us, together, powerful over what he became: a pool of scarlet, a maggot feast.

And when the community priest led us in the Lord's Prayer at our father's funeral, you stopped after "Who art in heaven." Then I stopped after "Hallowed be thy name." The two of us stopped together, amidst a mumbling congregation. You fixated on the candelabras to the left of the sermon podium, afraid that everything else would feel your escape. I fixated on you, Carlisle, because you meant more to me than truth ever could.

We didn't care to know the details afterward, and neither of us waited to find out. You with your suitcase of warmth, and me. I didn't get nearly as far as you, my dear Carlisle. You seemed to fall right out of existence, but I know that is just your way of hiding.

Missus is back in my room, silently gazing at the leather of this journal with a frustrated scowl. I keep trying to convince her that I had you, but she shakes her head and assures me I was alone, and always have been – just me, our father, and Mama. She shakes her head, her smile tilted with amusement, as she tells me the red was on my hands.

Extraordinarily powerful and deeply creative. There's a distinctive flair here that keeps it from the melodrama such stories often steer toward.

For the Fire

Mother split the river's ice.
The water surged a colloidal breath.
The house dark, a spoiled negative,
needing light, needing heat.
We loved the air: the swirls of
cedar bark and perfect sunshine.
There wasn't any other way, so
Mother split the river's ice and,
together, we found. Our feet
slipped through the stream, stirring
as we stole wood for the fire.
The water surged a colloidal breath.
The house puffed darkness and smoke.
The burn.
The burned.
The burning.
The house heats like a lover.
Whose woods these are I think I know.

✱

The language and imagery in this poem are beautiful. I love the new and apt descriptions of water, air, and fire. I can smell the smoke here.

Sailboat

    poisoned to the
               fibers we wove together
    fifteen years in the factory
    we worked up a
          sweat, now we
    have found this toy sailboat
       tiny plastic insignificant sailboat

    we negotiate it into
    the pocket of our faded rags
                and draw out the lint

    we are poisoned to the fibers we wove
    in this factory – this Indian factory
          crematory
                     factory

    where we bred threads and thimbles instead of children –
    no sparkling eyes tied up
          to the docks   of their sockets
    calling us mama, but
    tarnished eyes of a master whispering
               girl
                      Indian girl
                         slave
           girl

                      poison

LaBerge has captured that elusive atmosphere of an almost accidental journey, and, rather than feeling spoon-fed by the repetition, the reader experiences the redundant images as a gallery of snapshots. The piece subtly progresses from almost quaint ("we worked up a / sweat together, and now we / have this sailboat") to a haunting sort of deadness.

Hannah Toke

Fine Arts Center, Greenville, SC

Fleeting

after Gwendolyn Brooks

How could we have predicted it was you
who would settle in thick solitude, have
nothing of childhood memories but the thin blanket, thrown
over the back of your Pa's old chair, the one you made me
yours in. I'll never forget the feeling, after you scraped
me – a blunt shovel hitting rock two feet under, and me
staring out the window at birds flying past your shoulder with
a sour pain low in my abdomen. I thought of your
mother, trading sex for a Buick, as your mouth formed a kiss.

Instead of lamenting or exalting love, this piece takes a realistic stance on it. Like most things in life, there is good in the bad, and bad in the good. Superbly impressive. It has that attitude and that resentment that just makes great poetry.

Roots

When you first find yourself burning in the "flames" of love, it is probably unwise to mention the fact that you quite possibly are a pyromaniac. How cliché, and your Mother and Father, working back to back, chop iceberg lettuce and drizzle raspberry vinaigrette over the tall chunks. Both refuse to speak until the knives have been set down. They carefully step away from the counter, wash their hands, and get started on the roast.

When I think of my family, I think of my family tree. Not as in the picture where you fill in the names of your ancestors and relatives but as in a literal tree, in the lot where my Grandmother's old house used to be. It's an oak, and there are still three clothes lines hanging from the side of the trunk, leading to a pole that I used to run around as a kid. I believe it was planted right around my father's birth, maybe earlier, but it grew behind the deck of the little brick house. Most of my relatives' initials are carved around a knobby hole where a branch used to grow until it extended too close to the garage shed. In a large patch of grass, that tree is the only reminder of where the house's foundation stood. The house was in a flood zone, and so the county forced the entire block to relocate and settle elsewhere.

John Toke: "Why live here? This is where my dad brought me, and you tend to stay where you know. It's… It's hard to – hard to do different things in a familiar place. Especially here."

Brian and I sit in the front seats of his Ram 1500 truck, watching the pouring rain distort the windshield. We eat the frozen berries we had saved for dessert after burgers. The weather had changed suddenly, and we'd had to put off unloading the boat into water to reach the island we camp out on. I had snagged the bag before getting too drenched, fearing I would get hungry before the rain let up. We both push raspberries and grapes in our mouths in our boredom, listening to the drowning noise of falling water on the roof of the car.

I ask Brian, "So, how's Christa?"

"Don't know, don't care. I'm sure wherever she is, it's far from Greenville."

I pause to swallow a whole grape; a small ache remaining after it squeezes down my throat. "And how are you?"

He slips the tip of his pinky finger into a raspberry, his eyes squinting down. "Shitty… If there's one thing in the world I pray you never feel… it's this."

Q: Did you believe you would find the one?
A: "Oh, not at all… the one person for me theory? I didn't think that. I just think there are multiple people for everybody, you know?"
Q: How would you summarize marriage in three words?
A: "Um, it's three words. No – it's four… In it to win it."
Q: That's five words?
A: I used the same word twice.

The back doors of the house are open; the sun seems to pool like a puddle along the carpet floor, leaking. Mother is usually in the back yard, getting the earth stuck to her knees and her fingernails blackened with fertilized soil. The herb garden is flourishing and the bees hum past ears until they finally bump, a muted collision, with the side of your face. For the next hour, you will grip at your neck and wish to be touched in such a way that your ears vibrated.

"How's Peru?
Mr. Lewis Jones: "It's up some days… It's down others."
Today, up or down? Why?
Mr. Lewis Jones: "It's a Monday – self explanatory."

If I could describe my Grandmother's house, and everything me be stripped from the walls, I would say the words: Yahtzee, thin nightgowns, shoe polish, deer heads, crushed aluminum soda cans, turquoise velvet, chocolate rabbits, gasoline stains, and brass knick knacks. I would find these leaves in the backyard that were fuzzy, like dandelions, and put my hand against them. The leaves bigger than my hand – its fingers triangular and pleasing.

My father comes up to me one day wearing one of those fisherman hats with flaps and says, "Glad you've graduated from the 'what if' stage of your life. I almost went crazy. Almost."

What if Mom grew tentacles?
What if the moon could be lassoed closer?
What if we were driving, and a squirrel wouldn't move?
"We'd move on, honey."

Before getting started on a long drive down a winding Greer road in a Chevrolet truck listening to country music and sucking on a Coca-Cola soda…
In the beginning, it was our clothes we wanted to unbutton and shed. I knew it for what it was – a learning experience, a fresh face to study and observe. I remember thinking the end of the affair was timed, planned and calculated in a cold, affectionate

gaze, but then soon forgotten. It was not a sudden shift when we fell; it was not even jagged. Sometime after he began asking and I began giving, I stopped counting the days I had left with him. Sometime after that, he gave back in return. We are unbalanced, yet at our full capacity. We are our own keepers.

Mr. Lewis Jones: "What was your question again?"

What makes the home? Is it the place in which you live? or is it the people closest to you in any location?

Mr. Lewis Jones: "The people one."

So… women… to be cliché, do you think we differ from males in the whole wavelength idea, or is there over-thinking on any genders part? Does that even occur to you?

Mr. Lewis Jones: "What a bomb, throwing that one out there like that."

"I think that is just the idea, there's always unbalance, but I tend to ignore it, one because of pure laziness, the other, because the wife… there's just some things left unspoken."

How's the air over there?

Mr. Lewis Jones: "Well, it's 9000 feet above sea level, so the air is a good bit thinner. People get nose bleeds here too, but I get migraines, which will go away eventually. At least I don't get the shits, like other people did – it's the most common side effect of moving down here. You get used to it after a month, and I've got two more weeks to wait it out."

"Oh, and I sure don't mind the whole refraining from exercise part – That's nice."

Overcup Oak:

Usually a small, irregular tree with crooked or twisted branches; occasionally reaching 100' in height and 2' to 3' in diameter above a buttressed base, but usually much smaller; the crown is characteristically irregular and open, the root system shallow and widespread.

Habitat. A bottom-land species commonly occurring on poorly drained, clay soils subject to prolonged inundation; most generally associated with willow, water and swamp chestnut oaks, persimmon, elms, green ash, and waterlocust. -Guide to Southern Trees

…Good, bad, whatever – Just a memory that comes and resonates in your head.

Jacob Sheets: "They are harder to remember, the good ones… I remember… I remember when the power went out in oh-five… During winter break…"

The fireplace, Sarah, falling in love?

Jacob Sheets: "Yes. The night Rach spent the night… that was more of a fluttering feeling, like, 'this has to be a dream' kind of feeling the entire night. When the music was just right…"

Is love something tangible, solid, to you? Can you move it around and use it as an action instead of an internal expression? Can you do both?

Jacob Sheets: "I think it's untouchable….you can't want to love someone and it happen. It doesn't work like that, but I'm sure you already know that. I think of love… as a wild animal… a fire. Cliché, I know."

Something is broken in the room, yet we cannot know what it is. The nuts have been digested, yet the shells linger on the end tables, rolling, unsettled by the air. It is safe to conclude that the broken thing is wet and warm, like a weighted sponge, but it is not a heart. Often times we can hear it for a moment when the window unit dies down, sometimes not. If it is raining, we can never hear the sound, and it cannot hear us. The broken sound it makes keeps the stew simmering in the kitchen, and all doors ajar.

I'm sitting on the edge of a clay orange shore in the middle of Lake Kiowee. The stars are condensed, packed into the night sky's belly as if attracted to the water pulsing at my feet. The front legs of my camping chair are sinking, and soon enough I'm looking down at the angle of my fishing line disappearing into the dark lake. Brian, my uncle, feels as though this is a proper moment to tell me about his divorce. I count the shooting stars as he talks, and then he tells me about how long they last before the atmosphere burns them into dust.

�֍

The melding of genres and interweaving of personal story into the fiber of this literary nonfiction piece reminds me of Joan Didion's writing; such risk here didn't seem like it was trying too hard, though. It's clever, it has moments of beauty and humor, and the imagery is simply masterful.

Lila Thulin
Rowland Hall, Salt Lake City, UT

Percussive

Seal his eyes, crimson wax bursting
solid over feather-pale eyelashes,
so though blinded, he will know by sound
the sunset and sunrise, the coppering
of the star found in bursts of E minor
and silenced birds. From cut-crystal moments –
wine-glass chimes and yellow silk whispers,
too-sweet roses (petal edges blackened),
heavy paper, dial tones – he'll learn language,
scrolling words defined but phrases mutable.
Heartbeat's cousin, when steady pulse
takes pitch for a flashing second preserved,
lightning bug beating at glass with sputtering
wings. The inhale is forgotten in the wait
for the harp-string clarity of a beginning
before the tumble and leap reach two ends.
Now, held in the grace note before the fall,
his throat and fingertips are mirror-edged.

I just emailed this poem to myself so I could print it out and pin it on my desk. It's complex and interesting and musical and flirtatious and imaginatively wrought and just...wonderful. I love the images and the colors and the certain claustrophobia of fireflies in jars. I would fight for this poem.

Lila Thulin

Honey and Vinegar

I believe in abrasion
The harsh rasp of shovel and concrete and clenched
Hands, crystal glasses unstacked, the bitter
Tang of orange zest, kitchen counter accusations,
And the scrawl of ink that leaves an end half-finished.

I am too afraid of the fire to melt;
Toasted and burnt do not have enough in-between.

When I bake I use glass and metal so they beat my presence,
A declaration spelled in a Morse code of chops and scraping.
My grandmother knows this language only in echoes,
She kneaded sticky dough, painted with chocolate,
Dusted wood with flour like marble dust fallen,
And kept honey in a sticky-rimmed jar above the stove
So it couldn't crystallize, become too rigid to consider sweet.

Bees make puncture wounds because honey heals the holes
Made, how it falls into flour waning but does not cease.
It would bandage the buzzing under my feet and smother
The wing beats of my eyelashes, patch crystal, and sweeten.

This one has a soul that I love. It has personality and zest and propulsive rhythm reflected in its verbs. There's also a nice, subtle maturation in mindset that, coupled with that last stanza, keeps you turning it in your head over and over again.

61

Julia Tompkins

Saint Ann's School, Brooklyn, NY

When it Got Cold Out

When it got cold out Dad taught us how to build a fire –
he sent us out for kindling and made sure we wouldn't
shrink away from the flame. He put his hands – nothing like those hands –
around ours and told us when to flick our wrists, so the match would light.
The January it didn't snow we lay down the biggest logs we could find
at the bottom of our in-ground swimming pool. The reflection of the
flames sprayed orange water across the blue concrete. It was frigid in that orange water.
Nothing makes you cold like fire where water calls home.
Dad ordered a wood-stove from the Sears catalogue. It came
the twenty-seventh but he still put a bow on it and pushed the box
towards the barren tree. He said we would build fires inside and for
two months our living room smelled of cedar wood he got special from California.
We went to Florida, once, right after I turned ten.
On the beach he'd peel his navel oranges, and the fiery juice would glisten on his chin
with a citrus sweat as he bit into them, dropping the bright orange skin down
between his knees where it collected on the sand.
He used to say you could build a fire out of anything;
they'd told him that, back in the day, when he was an Eagle Scout.
The summer I went away to college, he burned our names in a cedar plank.
He burned our two names and said that nothing leaves a mark like
fire.

*

The language of this piece is quiet, but like the images in the poem, it's on fire. The understated passion behind the piece creeps up on the reader and becomes the invaluable driving force for a poignant coming-of-age poem.

Lillian Fishman
Weston High School, Weston, MA

How to Keep Your Sister's Secret

Leave the radio on at night. Don't listen to the way the gravel crumples below your window like paper airplanes in the wastebasket, like cereal. Keep your eyes out of the lake of light squeezed by the curtains onto your sheets; hold yourself bottled in the plum air and sing to yourself that you're dreaming.

Fall out of love with doorknobs. Remember the way they used to drink in light, the way they mirrored your baby lips and narrowed your face into a slim line, all the hours you spent watching the spinning silvered colors. When your sister turns the knob to your room, leans into the doorframe, when the lock scrapes against its niche inside the paneling, decide that you do not love the doorknob or the clean lock. Do not say to your sister, I love you. Wait and sing that you're dreaming in the purple hush of your secret throat.

The shoes, the sheets, the knob, the whisper, the lock, the falling, the flood. Listen to your sister's breathing slow after she turns off the radio. Give up and let the moonlight wallow in your skin. In the morning, stay in bed late to give her time to wash her face, clean her shiny shoes and hide them in the closet. Wait until the shower's running to push yourself up in the sheets and feel the mess of your hair. Don't turn the radio back on. Don't rest your hand on the doorknob's smooth ribbons and wait for it to warm under your fingers. That is done.

When you loll downstairs in the morning, don't meet your mother's eyes. Pour yourself cereal and the last of the milk. Survey yourself in the window's shallow reflection and wish, again, that your face were longer, your lips fuller. Think about yourself. Think of nothing to say when your mother says "Emma," and fathom that there is such a thing as silence, that you don't have to answer. Don't tell your mother what you're thinking. Don't tell her what you dreamt. Don't tell her of your love affair with doorknobs.

Wait for your sister to whisper to you because you're twelve almost thirteen and you already hear her when she comes in at night while the radio's on. Wait for her to tell you why she's wretching in the dark, why she's crying, why her eyes are black. Don't say to her, I love you. When she smiles at you, pretend you don't know. Lock the door when you shower to feel the complete aloneness. Relish, when you are bored, the quick pulse of harboring a secret. Handle doorknobs only with the tips of your fingers. Buy more milk. Take out the trash so your mother doesn't see the bright carcasses of your sister's pregnancy tests. Straighten your hair and cut off the parts that burn with kitchen scissors. Steal your sister's mascara. Put it back because you feel sorry for her and you aren't scared of her anymore but she doesn't know that she's powerless and you don't want to break her heart. Borrow her shiny shoes on Saturday morning and walk at the edges of the carpet in the hallways. Put them back in the closet. Notice the way your breath in silence is blue in the dark and wine-stained in the kitchen, unfurling like oil in water. Leave the radio on at night. Wait for the doorknob to wheel, unhurriedly, for your sister to spill in.

When she says to you, this time, "Emma," don't move. Keep your eyes out of the lake of light collecting in your pillow.

When she says to you, "awake?" don't let your lips twist. Don't tell her, I love you.

When she puts her hand on your shoulder, when the sheets kiss, when her hair traces a fishnet on your eyelids, don't put your palm over her knuckles. Keep still. Sing to yourself that you're dreaming.

Think of all of the times you have answered questions with nothings when you didn't know that silence was an answer while your sister rummages in the wastebasket. Think of the scratches in your sister's shiny shoes from the crumpling gravel like paper airplanes while she tears open another purple paper box, pees in the bathroom, while the radio ebbs into commercials. Think of her narrow face and her full lips when she says "Emma," because otherwise you will answer her. Think of the estranged doorknobs.

Knead your thumb into the skin of your wrist so your breath won't catch when she says "Emma, please."

Pretend that you do not hear your sister flinging the box and the stick into the wastebasket where they mewl against the plastic. Feel the floor shudder as she floods onto the bed, as she loosens and sinks into the cavern of the covers. Hold yourself bottled under the sheets. Don't tell her, I love you. Let her think you fell asleep with the radio on.

✱

The narrative distance Fishman creates in this piece is ingenious; she connects with the reader, but in such a detached way that you can get the sense of jadedness and abrasiveness but still accept that she is actually telling you these things that she would normally keep quiet.

Lillian Fishman

Fresh

The new house is all straight
even bones, no muscle yet.
There are loose stones
in the drive, near the stump of the tree
that stood at my window's elbow
when the great gloomy ghost
of the Eldridge house
first swallowed us, almost
acquiescent, too tired
to object. Too many floods,
maybe, too many fires
in the little blue grate.
The tree was first to go.
August and I lay in the grass
on a night there were no stars, only
the lake's eerie purl
but August has been buried
with the teeth of the Eldridge house
and that one night
when the stars knew better than to show.
They have survived.
Here, my mother says. The house
is only a newborn, already the culprit
of my loss.
Won't it be beautiful?
And the banister, and the soft windows
with the husked paint, I say. Gutted?
We're starting fresh
my mother says
to the lake, who has drowned too many daughters
to remember August.

I love that the Eldridge house is personified by literally becoming a person – a person with bones, muscles, teeth – so much so that I began to have a deep empathy for this inanimate object.

The Farm

after Gwendolyn Brooks

You are no longer mine I know I shouldn't tell you I
have loved you more than any girl yes I am
still at the pasture knees on the February grass a
furrowed, unbroken thing. I clutched at woman
hood on your moors that one night I told her who
she loved, but I am still the girl you know who hurries
home to catch the hard moon as it wakes through
your field, the place I watched white ankles in her
boyfriend's tuxedo shoes and breathed my prayers.

✻

Yes. Love the tone of this – it fits with the line it emulates so perfectly that it's as though "I am a woman who hurries through her prayers" is a secret message. This author seamlessly used the GS form to enhance her poetry. It's a gem.

Caroline Hamilton
Fine Arts Center, Greenville, SC

Wilted Grass and Interstate Lines

The yellow pastels in my mother's dress –
she drives too fast. When we left, she handed me the map,
told me to pick out a town, like shoe-shopping
or buying a new brand of toothpaste.
I closed my eyes and pointed

to someplace between the Boxcar Children
and Charlotte's Web, where the blue lines
on the atlas extend farther and farther
away from each other, as if stretching after a nap.

My mother plays Joni Mitchell on repeat.
I imagine the place we are going will have corn
and breathing room between the buildings,
but it might just have a Waffle House
and three trailers. It is impossible to tell.

The freeway is the same everywhere, glaring green
exit signs and overgrown medians.
The town we look for never appears,
and each exit ramp leads to the same pavement.
Yellow lines dizzy us.

We must have passed it, we must have missed it,
we must have gone right through it.
But this is not it and Joni Mitchell is Blue,
or so she says, and my mother has leg cramps.
The leather seats make me sweat,

Caroline Hamilton

and I have started to see pictures in the highway lines
of the map, the creases so deep
I am afraid to touch them.
My mother brakes when the road runs out
and rubs her knees, floating circle kneecaps.

We end nowhere – some beach in California.
There are cliffs and high waves. There is no corn.

❋

There's something almost raw about this piece, despite its precise construction. Great imagery, great voice, a sure sense of language and balance between writing and voice. The journey of it makes the poem feel like it's really moving. It's sweet and eloquently written. I'm a sucker for parent-child relationship pieces.

In the Winter

We found a dead dove on the front stoop. It was gray and crusted over with ice, the size of a lemon. We poked its swollen stomach hoping some leftover juices would spurt out, but none did. We took it inside and put it in the soup pot and hid it on the shelf in the closet. The next day, when mother asked us where her pot was, we told her that father had sold it to pay for the new window. So she made soup in a pan and left it to boil over onto the burner, drip down the front of the oven and leave a sticky film. She made father clean it up. We went upstairs and peered under the lid of the pot. There was a puddle of water from the ice and the bird seemed to have swelled. We figured it was holding its breath.

We named it Peter, thinking this would bring it eternal rest, and made a routine of checking on it. After it shed its feathers, leaving them fluffy and fragile against the dark iron of the pot, we saw how thin it was without its winter down. We stroked its stomach, so raw and brown and stretched and told each other we could feel a heartbeat, but it was just the pulsing in our fingertips. We tried resurrection anyway. We closed our lips between the edge of the pot and the lid to try and keep in as much of our words as possible as we whispered all the prayers we knew: *Hail Mary, Our Father, Glory Be,* hymns we remembered singing in church. We made crosses and fish out of tall grasses and wire and dropped them in the pot.

Everyday, during school, we would fill up the margins of our paper with crude drawings of the bird in thick pencil, trying to capture its crooked neck, the serene weightless chest, the stillness that at any moment could awake. The other boys in the class stared at our drawings and laughed. So we dragged them to our closet and opened the pot. The bird's bloated organs were visible through its skin and the boys cringed. The rot had begun to smell. We told them to talk to it, bless it, present it with a token. The boys removed their hats. We all stuck our mouths around the rim of the pot and whispered the *Gloria Patri*. Then we emptied our pockets: marbles, aluminum candy wrappers, ticket stubs, change from lunch. We put the lid back over it all and individually pressed our lips into the pot, mumbling proverbs and lullabies we remembered from childhood. Reverence.

When it was over, we all hoped that the bird would burst forth from the pot and fly into the air, some kind of new world phoenix, but doves can't rise from grass crosses and pennies. We placed the pot back on the shelf in the closet and filed out silently. Mother was downstairs in her green stained apron burning toast and she watched the boys leave.

She put the toast around the table and told us to come to dinner. After the soup pot disappearance, she had begun to burn everything. Probably because the new window had never come. She didn't speak to father about it, didn't speak to him at all; instead she cleaned the house religiously, telling us to clean ourselves the same way, rub until the skin comes off.

She didn't approve of the other boys coming over, with their muddy shoes and improper grammar. She felt the urge to clean them. But they came weekdays after school and stood around the pot, too frightened to lean into it and whisper. We took the lead and started off with the songs and verses we already knew. Soon though, we made up our own prayers, things like: *we believe in resurrection and hollow bones, the unreachable embrace of sky and land. We believe in the freedom of birds. Birds. Birds. Birds.* We didn't approve of the boys' lack of participation and asked them to leave if they couldn't bring themselves to communicate with the bird. Only one of them was forced out before the others straightened up and began bringing small objects to place in the pot. We told them the Bird was grateful. Whether out of fear or true dedication, the boys started to whisper table blessings and nursery rhymes into the pot. We said this would fill them with the energy to fly. They mumbled among themselves and tried to believe. On their own time, they made wings out of wax paper and glue. They brought them to the house when they came, strapped over their shoulders like school bags. We tried to make our own, but mother refused to give us the wax paper and told us to clean behind our ears. The boys took our lack of wings as lack of enthusiasm and staged a coup, grabbing the pot by its large handles and tugging it toward the door. We fought back. The bird had always been ours. There was a struggle, a broken nose, but we all gave up at the same time, letting the pot clatter to the floor, lid fly across the room, the putridity of dead things emanating in a thick column up to the ceiling. Bugs previously unnoticed began maneuvering out of the pot, climbing over the rim and exploring the floorboards with their antennas and legs. The contents of the pot seemed to be aiming for a stew consistency and the bird could no longer be seen under all the gifts we had left there. The boys stood for a moment, then removed their wings in silence and placed them over the top of the pot. They carried it outside to the backyard and dug a hole in the ground with their hands. We watched them place the pot in the ground while we stood at the upstairs window, clutching the lid. They filled the hole in and put their wings back on their shoulders. We did not see them again.

The next day, the scent still lingered in our room and mother came up to dispel it. She sprayed all the perfume she owned and placed fresh herbs around the room. She said it must be those mongrel boys, she always smelled it when they were around, that we were not to see them anymore; smells catch. We sat on the bed, staring at the closet, holding the lid between us. Later, when she called us to dinner, we went downstairs and ate burned eggs.

We hung the lid on the wall and brushed against it every morning, hoping for luck or blessings or good will. We spent more of our time looking out the window, at the patch of brown soil that covered the bird. We decided we had to rescue it. There was not the problem of shovels, we used our hands like the boys, blundering in the night to the hole, now just an indentation in the grass. We dug until we lifted the pot out, much heavier now that it was filled with dirt. It packed under our fingernails and into the creases of our sleeves as we scraped out the mud.

When we finally reached the bird, it was crushed against the bottom of the pot, the tears in its skin releasing its guts into the mix of tokens we had left with it. Cradling the bird with our fingertips, we lifted it out of the pot, mesmerized by its closed eyes, bent wings. We stood close to each other as if we had the chills, and held the bird in our hands, staring at it until we thought it had taken flight, left our hands weightless. The resurrection we had been waiting for.

✱

Beautiful. There's a nostalgic tenderness to it that really gets me. It's just subtle enough. From the first person plural narration to the religious imagery and relationships between characters, it feels honest, like it's not trying to be anything it's not.

Rose Miles
Saint Ann's School, Brooklyn, NY

Sulfur Dreams

When you were once sick in bed,
I nursed you. Hot broth colder towels
You told me about a dream you had that
Chased you. Of something you were unable to outrun, to outsmart.

When I crack eggs I can never break the shell in an even line.
Even tempo even tempered
Even you, passing through the kitchen to stand in front of the fridge for an hour
Would laugh.

You mentioned casually one day,
barely recovered, you had a
vocation. Your calling was a mission in
Uganda and you heard it screaming.

Your mother told me once after Monday dinner, between dessert and baby pictures
That when you were a child you ran around the house naked.
Over breakfast I asked you if you knew what erosion was. Disintegration. dissociation.
You were quiet, but when we were brushing our teeth you broke the silence
foamy-mouthed to tell me you think you knew what I meant.

✱

I love the narrative here and the way this author so skillfully weaves these ideas together to create a cohesive poem. And I love those little observations of life (e.g. "When I crack eggs I can never break the shell in an even line.") that work so well with this piece.

Season of Infertile Seeds

juice turns and churns until it is moaning –
the squish of grapes under our feet,
seeds bursting into our eyes until
they are dehydrated and
we are deprived of warmth.
small seeded tears like jam fall slowly and stickily,
depositing juice into your cheeks;
you have been preparing for hibernation.
you shake and stomp the bliss from the
grapes until you are ready for winter.

the long shadows of shorter days
seem to make you longer, leaner.
leaning against the barreled bucket,
you remember the oaky chardonnay
once made here.
and you, my Atlas, have lifted the trees
from their roots and carefully separated
the stems and seeds and we are
deprived of growth.
our crop, deprived of witness
of its own.
sweetly sucked and ready to freeze.

This poem eloquently tells a simple story of a winery, but it tells so much more. With phrases like "you shake and stomp the bliss from the/grapes until you are ready for winter," this piece speaks to the fleeting nature of childhood and innocence. The writing is chilling and simple; it's got me hooked.

Anna Feldman

Fremd High School, Palatine, IL

This is Not Catharsis

You should know right off the bat that this is not catharsis. I've talked and cried about it more than I care to. So I'm not getting it all out; don't feel like you're doing me a favor, because I'm writing this for you. All I ask is that you put aside your judgments and listen. There is a moment when you hold that pill bottle in your hands. There is an instant when you decide to die and everything's in place. You were once indifferent about living or dying; now you actively desire death. All the suffering, all the tiredness, all the headaches will go away. You'll be at peace. You are at peace. The cutting and starving, that was out of loathing, desperation. But this is something else, something peaceful. It's merciful.

It took you six months to get to this moment. It started out as a whisper coming from the edge. The edge where monsters roam and dangerous girls play. At the beginning, the edge has its glamour. It tells you maybe you shouldn't eat so much. Start counting calories, at least. Work out just a little bit. And you listen, because you want to be sexy and dangerous. You're just a girl. You want special. The edge calls and you don't any know better but to take a step forward, toward your whisper. Toward your personal monster.

The monster is your friend. It keeps you hungry and empty. It makes you strong. But disobey: eat, stuff your face, bloat like a puffer fish. It doesn't like that. And you're closer now, so close that it can reach your arms and stick your nails into your stomach. Ugly stupid fat bitch, it says. Ugly stupid fat bitch but this makes up for it, just a little bit. And you release your nails and wipe off the blood. And you smile because you're so close to the edge, to destruction. Days later your fingers burn because you want more, more. And then you find a shard of glass.

Ugly stupid fat ugly stupid bitch. Its words give you fuel, rocket power in your arms to slice up your hip. That's another moment, when you reach it. A checkpoint, if you will, on our journey to the end. The high point of the cut, the gasping pain, the icy euphoria. You tingle all over and your vision sharpens. Your body is so cold. It's frozen desire, the purest form you've ever felt. And the monster croons hate words and praise words simultaneously, ugly stupid fat yes strong fat pure bitch strong. Because it's proud of you. It's in your blood now.

Before long, you don't sleep well. You lie in bed in the late hours of the night and the monster creeps up your veins and into your head. You're so close to it, you can taste it. This is the first murmur of death. Because you can't live on the edge anymore. It's calling and it takes so much to fight it. So much. The monster has lost its glamour and stares at you with its distorted face. You lose desire and now you're just afraid. Afraid, tired, and alone.

Shake the pills, one two three times. Turn the bottle upside down and hear the rush.

This is for you. You who says that everyone gets sad sometimes, who says that you don't sleep sometimes either. This is for you who says that you just need a couple of pills and you'll be okay. This is for you who can't understand and doesn't want to, for you because you need to understand me. This is for you who wonders if I'm crazy, a lunatic, if I hear voices. This is for you who wonders why any sane person would ever want to end her life. This is for you, for thinking that I'm making this up. Who says, of course you're not ugly or fat. Can't you see? Can't you see? Depression is real. Suicide is real. Ugly stupid fat bitch is my reality. My monster, the edge, the call, they're all my reality. And I learned I'm not the only one fighting them. Suicidal roommates, suicidal friends all playing Uno in the common room. So don't call us crazy, because something went wrong in our heads. Don't shun us or doubt us or think we're weak, because we're so strong. We wake up every day and we fight. We fight for our lives and our sanity while you're worrying about what you're going to eat for lunch. We're stronger than anyone can see.

So this is not catharsis. This is me taking you through my fight. And I fight it every fucking day. I fight the ugly stupid fat bitch ugly stupid from the moment I open my eyes until the moment I finally fall asleep. So don't you dare think I'm exaggerating. Don't you dare criticize me or the rest of us. Because we are just poor, desperate, tired, and strong beyond imagination. We are alive.

All I ask is that you put aside your judgments and listen.

�֎

It's raw, it's painful, it's honest. The words are as painful as what the author experienced, and the second person is jarring and hits home. While it's effective in showing the narrator's distance from what she experienced, it also makes the piece even more poignant for the reader. The fragments are punchy and honest. It's rare to see a piece this blatantly honest.

Joanne Koong

Orange County High School of the Arts, Irvine, CA

For the Next Woman You Meet

On your first date, ask him how good he is at chess. He'll say the humble thing, that he's absolutely terrible with a tendency to always get the colors mixed up. Don't believe him. Forty minutes and perhaps an empty wine glass later, he'll lean across the table and ask you with a trembling heart whether you play. Say yes.

Know how to play chess. Fall in love with the game more quickly than you fall in love with him. The third time he takes you to his apartment and tries to kiss you, tell him you like a chess player who knows how to mate.

When he takes you to a restaurant and asks you what you want to order, don't pretend you're a petite eater. Look at the menu, know what you want, and get it. This doesn't apply to just restaurants.

Don't drive thirty-six miles to his apartment on a Friday night drunk. Even if he opens his door as you try to slur I love you, he won't say it back.

On the 3 A.M. nights when he can't sleep, stay up and write love letters to strangers with him. Tell them about yourself. Say what you're trying to live for, what you want in life. Pour your heart into the page and then enjamb them between books or bus seats the next day. You'll learn how to be a humanist.

Know that when he takes you, in the middle of the night, to the courtyard of the town's abandoned church to whisper for you poetry on the verge of nihilism beneath the California stars, he's trying to say that he loves you.

Know that these moments will pass you by.

*

> Love is ephemeral. And that's hard to admit for all of us, but especially for the narrator in this piece. Her bittersweet, nostalgic struggle is touching and enthralling. A part of me has fallen in love with her love.

Joanne Koong

How to Read Neruda When Heartbroken on a Friday Night

after Gwendolyn Brooks

In this interpretation of his Twenty Poems of Love where all the
staggeringly profound lines are written for us and the only
love we need is in his corazon, his sober heartaching sanity
reminds us of how everything, especially time, is
both lost and gained in increments, in nights and moments where a
warm body embodied on a page can embrace us wholly and cup
our tears of insobriety with a tenderness only a poet can have, of
which we seek when we read Neruda while drinking a cup of Chilean tea.

✱

I love this piece. It plays off of Brooks' line, and it's also a commentary on Neruda. Still, it has a new level of depth by creating a heartbroken character who has these amazing insights into the poetry. Beautiful, compelling, and sophisticated. And that title is a gem.

The Sanguine Sovereign

Below smoldering eyes of black, Cupid's-arrow lips of red spit out ardent orders, sending her kingdom into a fray. She is a Queen in every sense of the word—watch how a fawning court carries out her every whim and desire. Was she always this regal? This cruel? Were her dreams of decapitation simply, perhaps, another example of her losing her head?

Observe the sparse little thing before her, blonde curls trembling under a black bow. How pathetic she seems next to that spectacle draped in luscious robes, rubies clinging to her pale throat. The two furrows twixt her eyes, those terrible scorching eyes, deepen as she hollers in the most regal fashion, "Off with her head!" Scepter pointed true, and blood-red mouth set in a curious smirk.

The command has been ordered; the deed is to be done. It is time to retire.

Clap softly now, let us not break her concentration. A master of the game she is, all the cards forever in her favor. Ah, look how the nobles tremble, fearing that today may be their lucky day.

What rage! What marvelous anger and angst revels beneath her crown! Could it be simple madness? Why heavens, no! Madness is for the poor, certainty not royal blood. 'Tis genius then! Twisted, but true. Perhaps a tinge of sadness has been added to the brew? Sadness over her roses, which grew white anew. Stubborn weeds! How dare they defy their sovereign. If it is red roses the queen desires, it shall be red roses the queen receives. Quickly now, one by one, prick your fingers and please the queen, prick your fingers and bathe the roses red once again.

Red as they were when she loved him, and he sang to her sweetly beneath the apples trees, heavy with their buxom fruit. Silence now! She might overhear! For her to remember the sharp taste of a fruit so godly and good would be a time for us to fear indeed.

The game is over, the dancing is to begin. She is at her crimson throne, enveloped in the favor of the divine; now stolid she is, unhappy once more, that smirk that once graced her dissipating along with the day.

Could it have been the loneliness? I beg your pardon? Before she was a queen she was child. A child! What a foolish thought! A queen is a queen form cradle to crypt; she is to be born fully equipped. But twixt that cradle and this crypt she was a child.

A child who roamed the castle halls searching for a crack in stone, marble, and glass, in between the chapels and ballrooms. Melancholy feet pit-pattering up and down, up and down. Undershirts and underskirts she searched, under coffers of gold and statues of silver, yet it was never found.

What was never found? What? Why, my dear, is it not clear – her heart, her soul, the one being she could never control.

Oh, but that was solved long ago. The search abandoned, a seamstress was called, and a new heart was made from thread and yarn of red, two reflecting question marks to match the ones in her head.

All rise, the Queen wishes to part! Bow and curtsy as is the way. Smile at your ruler supreme and her crimson flag that flies high, and never forget that she owns it – your heart that is. Locked away under mystical lock and key, though it seems the thousands do not replace the one she lost so very long ago. Smile, smile at your queen.

Never forget she is your queen – Queen of Hearts, that is.

�֍

This one definitely made my day. So romantically sophisticated, glittering in all the right places with scoffs and pouts and such foxy satire. Bewitchingly fun to read. It's flashy, it's mad, and sometimes so wretchedly melodramatic you're surprised you're still reading it, not to mention still very, very much believing in it.

Tina Zhu
Shanghai American School, Shanghai, China

Quiet is Her Favorite Fix

she is just a speck of static
in this disarray of people,
asphyxiated by the white
noise. quiet is her favorite fix

(she's picked her poison: loneliness.)
she sways unsteadily inside
a bathroom stall, with one hand to
the plaster wall, the other grasping
at the tails of her rising breath.
the people raise their winding scales,

their symphony around her but
the only thing she hears is diss-
onance. she is a dandelion
seed, swept up in a gentle gust,
an ache, when all she wants is to
withdraw into the umbra of

a desk and coil herself up
beneath like a knot of wires.
there are fires smoldering in
her throat, there are wisps of smoke and
confession leaking through her lips;
and she is just a pinhole star
left out of constellations drawn
in smooth and shifting lines of light

it's been three days and no one's called.

I absolutely adore this piece – a whirlwind of similes and imagery, beautiful and original, flashy and on display. It almost worries me that I like it so much. It's quick and windblown and I feel like I'm left plodding behind with my hands outstretched.

Raven Hogue
Oak Park & River Forest H.S., Oak Park, IL

Yazoo City

after Gwendolyn Brooks

Water bugs, beryl and brisk, were made of vinyl then.
Scratched the gospel in ochre under a
claw-footed tub. Great-grandfather's blood wilted in sickness.
He sucked his breath into a fist. The iron stove heaved
as they amputated his leg. Mercer churned within.

❊

I love the understatement here. A poignant, haunting piece. The end of it reminds me of Robert Frost's "Out, Out" (but slightly less morbid, strangely) — I love the idea of shocking you with the realization that this is about an amputation. And I love "sucked his breath into a fist."

Michelle Jia

Markham District High School, Markham, Ontario

Peter Visits the Kensington Gardens

I flew into the evenings like a bow-legged saint.
The things I got away with because your mother loved me:
hunger (too strong and too often), frequent blushing,
berry-spotting, Uxbridge.
That was when the water was round and ceaseless,
when the moss was an army of Peabody heads
and your hands were moon sculptures.
Cantaloupe strayed off the plate to join you.

I think now of the sounds before all,
the Bristol boats creaking at dawn
like a fleet of monsters about to set sail;
the obscene kissing of mud to our soles
and our souls. Highway at high tide.
Hail in the eaves.
I will always swear that I heard it,
your fingers speaking to the estuary.

Then Sussex pulled in and over
like a smuggling blanket, red-hot
the hour pinched and whiny.
There was shame of all kinds:
your eroding silhouette, Mother's tangled expression,
foot jammed on the gas. Travelling slow,
I was the answer to the road's question.
If you belonged to fever that held you –
it could have been then
that the green rictus of the future
made its nest in the faces of doves.

Your mouth became clear and beautiful, did you know?
Plant life came off your skin, hung glistening
from your ears. I followed the road in your hair
to some ivied wood; I became small and lost
and toxified. Still Merseyside drew itself up,
blew on the windchime of your sickness.
You swung creaky
and your face was the towering cliff
that I died against, over and over.

Bottles came onto the shore.
Your mother was a coat-hanger magician
who spooned the rocks down your throat
while I didn't ask for much, hanging on like linen
or leaves, secretly believing I was the cure.
Brighton came and went; so did my belief.
There is nothing more painful
than being so young.

You smelled like the pier some nights.
Disappearing into something immense,
your hands quaking and trimmed
beneath the vast implacable wetness.
This rose or that
evaporated off your skin, bruised
by the Oxford evening, by a larkspur star.
I was with you, did you know?
I wandered dutifully with no flashlight,
retired miracle worker. Stole out
as sleep closed your gate,
your murmurs following me like perfume:
To die would be an awfully big adventure.

Michelle Jia

I wanted anyway, to stay
and not just because I was allowed
and not just because the stars followed you
I will always want
I will always have wanted
even now to stay
I will always always
Do you understand?
You are not a garden
This is not about time.

�֍

This piece had me at "Cantaloupe strayed off the plate to join you." So gorgeous I can't stand it. Every time I read it I spot another absolutely radiant description. "Hanging on like linen or leaves" is possibly the most beautiful depiction I've ever read of someone who tries to be quietly, un-overbearingly supportive and relevant.

מרה (or, "Rebellious")

Maria, your puckering made me
reconsider, your gold-sheathed thighs
wrench-like, titanic, forged.
Maria, the valley that swallowed
the zebra herd was yours. All that hunting
did a number on your fingers.
All that claptrap is how you still make
your keep, transmuted by touch
into rice smells and pregnant
black beans for the morning.
What ghoulish promise led you here?
You scoff at your cerebral vacuole,
your own name a thin disguise
for a brand of fast food. Maria
Mini, Queen Maria, the Marian
Sea. When you speak, the birds weep
and tear their wings from their shoulders
like tropical leaves. Why stay where paint
will choke you? Where your lips will only memorize
the seven billion ways to pronounce a kiss?
Billowing saint, you faith-avenger, you are born
into language and you claw your way out.

✻

Damn. I love this piece. It's a battle cry and a shriek of pain and a song and a prayer. This modern ode-type deal is what I would want the nonexistent love of my life to nonchalantly slip in the pocket of my gold-sheathed pants.

Kathleen Cole
Fine Arts Center, Greenville, SC

Running of the Children

This is a time of intensity, of glass-breaking stares and lipstick smeared on girls' lips and imprinted on the faces of boys. Coats were stolen from cubbies, soccer balls aimed at faces. This was our legs kicking the air, arms pinwheeling. We thought of our bodies as compact and under our control at all times, though not wholly our allies.

We were the children; our aim was straight and our focus overpowering. Little girls and boys who, to one another, were not little. We were the other: our mothers proclaimed us innocent, ordered sheet birthday cakes to be devoured in square portions with plastic forks. Our mothers plotted, held meetings – what to do with the children? What to do with the small versions of themselves running amok, their own personalities laid bare in the streets? They baked incessantly; they could not find answers, but, as long as there was food, there would be meetings. They became swollen, bloated with their fear but they would not say it. They knew being afraid would give us power. We knew as well as they that we didn't need it.

We were the children of dissent. We begged our parents to get rid of the pets; we feared they would turn on us. Our parents began finding their food bowls and litter boxes left outside, the cat mewing at the door one night and gone the next. They suspected us but there was no proof. There would never be proof. But we alone knew the power there was to be found in numbers, in miniatures, in underestimation. We were the children and we always would be.

What of our fathers? The husbands who could have wrangled us, roped us with sheer strength, saved us from ourselves. Husbands always in transit – from home to work to more work to another kind of work to home to sleep to waking. Their power was to be found simply in momentum. Privately we consulted physics textbooks, plotted to stop them.

In the night we did not dream. Our mothers came into our rooms, asked to read us stories, asked to tuck the covers around our wriggling bodies. We had agreed that we would have none of it; for, if they began to read, we turned and talked among ourselves. We slept above the covers. They thought the worst was yet to come; we knew the worst was upon us and had been for some time. We could smell it when we walked around the soccer field at the school; some of us said we could see it in each other. It that we never voiced. It that made us afraid of our pets, afraid especially of infants. When our parents consulted, asked themselves why we weren't like the children they had been, the children they couldn't picture, we said we were preparing. If they would wait out the storm we would fight it, because we believed we could stop the storm in its tracks. Our bodies were our shells – our parents hid inside theirs and we inhabited ours, spread ourselves out, touched every part.

We knew the beginning of the storm was guaranteed; beginnings are always guaranteed. It was the end we were concerned about, the end that kept our heartbeats high and our toes warm. Endings were evasive – it was like eating soup with a fork. It could be done, but it would be drawn out and you would probably spill it on yourself.

And when the storm came we thought we would be ready. We thought we would know. We thought trumpets would announce it and we would feel it in our extremities and we would know to find each other. But what we found was what the storm had always been: we the children, our whirlwind hair and bodies like engines, thundercloud eyes, born to turn on ourselves.

�֍

Eerie and thought-provoking. Like nothing I've seen before.
The ideas of childhood it touches on are haunting and resonant.

Kathleen Cole

On the Island

after Gwendolyn Brooks

We've exchanged all the proper words, however
this leaves the empty space of the improper. I
have what I have –
You sip your milk white coffee and say you've heard
birds sing late at night, the way dogs sometimes cry, that
you never want it again. Sometimes
when you were young you crashed your tiny boats, you
slammed the bath toys until they rocked with waves. Have
I ever done that to you? Would I? Again it's to
the ocean, time to make a deal.
We watch the pelicans dive devilishly
into the briny water, come up with
fish still jumping in their beaks, drowning.

A mother's worst fear? They'll say men,
to make you laugh. They won't say how in
their own lives they've encountered worse – the order
of things is not what they've been taught to
teach you. She showed you how to swim
but not to sink like the fish, not to see them
in your bathwater at home. Not to
be afraid of everything, even the shore.

Love this one. The end just seals the deal for me; the perspective on a mother is a sophisticated, refined observation. So insightful.

While We Wait for Old Age

after Gwendolyn Brooks

I have not aged, says my
mother, since the last
crumbling line of defense
fell into what is
now your father.   The
dog won't bark – at present
her animal muscles are tense.
The adoption agency couldn't help it.
It's such a little
thing, but how it hurts
to watch a dog watch me.
I know now
that my mother went to
the church not to pray, but to know
how to ask.   How to ask for things, like I
need you to speak, maybe listen.   Shall
we dance, my father asked, once, not
to my mother.   One day we'll go
and get a real dog, find a cathedral
where we won't have to lament hunting
and all of the dead animals in
all of the world, even Spain.
We will teach my brother to say nor
and vice-versa, funny, cherry-
flavored foreign words, picking
them from a basket like he was in
an orchard. Cold like Michigan
autumns and raw, or
warm and wet – a summer spent in Maine.

The unnatural enjambment is deliberate and endearing here. It's a family portrait. Enjambment isn't always neat. Still it's beautiful. And Kathleen's exquisite use of the long line in a Golden Shovel poem makes me appreciate the challenge of the form even more.

Red Cowboy Boots

"Ma, Ma slow down." I stretch my fingers forward towards Ma's slippery hand and feel the Sinking Feeling again. Money from the wallet, money from Ma's heart. I am loved thirty-seven dollars less because of the red boots – not including tax. They hardly work properly anyways: won't walk fast enough, are as stiff and sweaty as heating pipes, and took money out of Ma's heart. Red. I should have known the boots would begin to look like butchered pelts on Chicago's melting July streets – streets smeared with chewed-up gum spit between black cracks. Red is a miserable color. Rojo. The first cowgirls were Mexican. I am a rose white cowgirl with bleeding feet and no pigtails. And broken boots. The seams on the black soles are fraying like the edge of Ma's love.

Was it worth it to ask?

Ma stood in the shoe store, a skinny tree trunk in a too big t-shirt and two dollar sandals with her arms crossed, and said "No." She said "No" because there was no money for them anywhere. Not in the wallet, not under the mattress, not in her back pocket. That is what she said. But they had glossy toes like mirrors that pointed from their tall shelf under the poster of that cowgirl on TV, and they were pointing at me. So I talked back with tears. One, two, three, one million quivering on my red-puffed cheeks, skipping over my gapped teeth.

Ma breathed low and hard through her nose in that way that said silently "I will love you a little less for this." But she took out the credit card, shiny, plastic-y, red. Red like the boots, like my puffed cheeks, like her heart, and gave it to the pale lady stuck to the pale wall behind the cash register. "That's thirty-seven dollars," she said, and Ma shriveled into herself a little more, fingering her empty wallet. "Do you know what this means?" she said to me. No, I shook my head. I was half listening, half absorbed in the new-smell of the rubber grips on my boots' soles.

"It means that I have thirty-seven less."

"Thirty-seven less what?"

"Thirty seven less to give you. Once you spend it, it's gone forever. Put the boots on and let's go," she said, tapping her foot and holding the credit card before her so that the silver words in the corner splintered department store lighting at my feet.

That is when the first Sinking Feeling came. I stared at Ma's credit card all blood red and pulsing as she held it there with her narrow wrist drooping to the side, letting it flutter above her left breast. And I realized where money comes from when there is none anywhere (not in the wallet, not under the mattress, not even in the back pocket). With Ma looking at me – credit card over her heart and sighing in that way that tells you little wisps of money-love are escaping through her teeth – that is how I found out.

And I spent it. I spent it before I knew it, and now it is sitting in the steely fingers of that cash register with the pale hands pushing the buttons. I am scared that the heart bank will sound a little empty now when I step in, and that my footsteps will hang lonely and cold from its ceiling. I am scared of that and I am sorry. I am a rose white cowgirl with bleeding feet and no pigtails and I do not want to be. And my boots don't work, although I wasted thirty-seven dollars of love on them and the bank is more empty now and Ma is a wilted tree and I am a balloon with the air let out who is being sucked backwards toward the gum in the black sidewalk cracks. Love is a hard thing to hold.

✸

It's fresh and unique, and it communicates a strong, multi-faceted, and sophisticated message in such an understated and simplistic way – the true mark of a strong writer.

I Keep You Alive in My Dreams

i keep you inside of me, chronic
& ill-fitting, sit sidesaddle on
bent lungs, glower, shift,
nettle me for always;
the movement, youth-led, melts
your starrynight moxie
but trust me, ennui is a flare of tight jeans
and you, Concrete Queen,
are a nude city sidewalk, sultry slew long-talk,
i toil the highways of Shyness and Rust
& you bust from a universally shit-upon shirt like
an underaged thumb, Jesus Will Jive For Our
Cinnamon-Lips, your voice will coerce me,
molest me (yes ayngel trust-me)
in moments of side-splitting
beauty be still –
let me wipe off the fluid, i'm ethereal mob
hunkered, studious and holy, dart round your
mouth – it is a Fake! they scream
i fucked up for certain but you're always
with sweetness unheard of beneath me   (deep breathly)
and follow :
you the penultimate criminal, choking
on the chic state of your guilt
and i in crimson
code dessert,   flaunting just-a-kidness,   will
hoard icky kisses & be well   surmounting hip-width (sit!)

i
wear
you
like
them   northern   lights
too paranoid to look, just look,
too sadlysoftly to acknowledge
an alien pink light
i stretch you studded like punk lyrics,
saturate me didn't write 'em
no one matters no one else knows what
whatwhatwhatwhat's the matter, Hun?

brace yourself

you brute well-rounded
femme oh-well; long-winded wino
got lost in the wash, i'll spend my life
approximating the exact length of your
lashes and percent of you that's wail,
that's grit, that's will – &ask

what
monstrous self-importance
is involved in thinking
that this life is the most interesting,
the dearest, the
sauciest thing in creation? hell,
the back of my neck

Brittany Newell

when i think of you gently
deciding your probe is enough to unzip me
of god and waste me like i, will be anyway,
inflate my brain til it veers littly girlish away
&tangles in the trees, sick orange, to be choked upon by sumthing
say,
stay, stay, stay with me
every arm i ever had will find the bad-spots on your back
and press you, bashful dictator, angelic turpentine, to lie
and fill a body emptied fresh
up up to fringe and fuck with speckled flesh of bad decisions
pelvic indecision (do we want a longgone meadow
or a melody to powder up n supersnort?
the drive
is awfully dull, i'm told…)

oh
delude me
love, you've got
the best seat in the house
but don't give in, don't
doze, don't dream of other scrawny homes, blonde curtains,
cats, with hearts less dense than mine, with taste, i swallow and
decide. i, i, i, i keep you brightalive, i fry you, i wrench you, i want you
to know, it is i, wet with sleeping, vernacular soft ly bleeding,
who keeps you,
o dreamboat
so rakish, in shortshorts,
karmic cheekbones, your drizzle
self-loathing
your bleached wit,
your trueness &fireblue tidbits,

Brittany Newell

your kiinky brand of forgiveness
your nose-broke atonement   ongoing
HeavyHearted   (beg pardon)
    i   know it

❋

This is a poem that I will be reading again and again. The rhythm is moving, the imagery is captivating, and the manipulate and twist of language and grammar makes for a great piece. I think both the style and content captures not only adolescence, but especially our generation's adolescence. It's rebellious, clever, passionate, snarky, and unapologetic.

Foreplay

The skinny girl with long rat hair
in sex is not submissive –
she is incapable of lying back,
she couldn't place the ceiling's color…
all soft parts of her, all-ears, react;
the finest hairs rise to mute summons
and she spirals with sopranic
focus, jangle wince inquire praise,
a torrid contradiction as
the red-hot elevators slam her chest
and the downy torment,
acid-tuned, slowly quartered, promises a pit:
the romance percolates to dust,
of a snortable variety
and feel! the sinister release,
the bigness that delays you –
no you'll never brown or curl now,
your beauty usurps tongue or tick,
flayed sunshine of an oft-used room
whose odor becomes part of you –
you do your best,
you sleep wallward and bathe in jest
your sadness, rimmed
by sleight-of-hand and lacy grit,
is a scoliotic mystery
shit-shingled in your favor: oh that braid
is something else. Forgive her her
consistently wrong timing and a taste
for laceration (some say it's in the
primeval job description) Twist
a little closer to the precipice,
its mauve bent and sense-of-loss swell
up like lips, intoning, are you sure?

are you sure you want to know?
Things could be simple could be
dulled: are you sure you have the time to wait
for certitude, indecent flowers blackly bunched
in piquant jars, to grow?
You-boy sigh against the glass. This shyness'll be the death of us,
the blaze of bridges on that brow, as lovely as is weary;
the skinny girl, on sheets, drinks all,
while the brusque attention of a hand
induces shivers, shitty dreams,
and pause (less blonde, more bone)
to follow pause.
        Broken-horsed, she foils; enter blandly as a breeze
        and leave that midnight om-chant to the dogs.

This poem just sucker punched me in the best way possible.

Brittany Newell

She Combs My Gnarled Hair in Record Time

my mother feeds me absinthe
dig?
                    she blinks atomic modesty
her breast is coffee-stained, like thought,
hard-pressed against terse windowpanes
her brow is marked & circledby
the stormy joint of time…
a dizziness precedes her
when I try to talk of drugs: she turns
like futile spring, the yellowed optimist,
she sings a tricked-out diddy & conducts
with her third eye(i spy…on constant
bathtubs of hers…rainbo-water won't stop running down
the ruddy walls of A Warm Gun)she
reaches out her "waving" hand, who summ
times doubles as a knuckle-smudging-ketchup   or
a brushing-hair-out-of-my-shyness   hand,   as
we stroll around the kitchen(semislept in)
laughing to enhance
the speed at which   debatably blonde hair grows –
casting offbeat pecks
toWards the window (rusted   steamy   round,
like the face of schoolgirl-enemy)
she lets the wayward weeds grow thick, she
admires their
Tenacity…
The days are getting weirder but
it only makes us right :
we drink our drinks with fingers linked
& lightly breathe the perfume of
subversion, thinking, "thank you godd
                    for awl i've got,"

our eyes affixed to the bald window, waiting,
waiting for the whisper, that will justify It all –
she says to me,   voice flush with love,

the fungus in the garden has the color of tanned flesh.
i wish you saw
the sun more.
          sipping lanterns,
          we digress.

✱

I want all my moments to be written like this, whimsical and quiet and real. When people talk they don't just start and stop and Have A Conversation, and Brittany Newell knows that completely.

Traces

When I brush my teeth I know what my pussy tastes like.

Don't let your mind automatically go there – I've got boyfriends and an adroit hand if it should come to that. It's just one of those things. Standing wet-haired at the sink in an old T-shirt I can taste the inside of my body, chest loosened and hips giving slightly with each genius stroke.

I used think it might be the repetitive brushing motion, or the nearness of my body to nakedness at nighttime, freshly-lotioned and worn-in by the mandatory sunlit hustle, but now I know it's something subtler, something between me and the steamed mirrors. It's something more attuned to the tiny sting of blood in the slits between my teeth when I push the brush too hard too long and point my eyes towards the ceiling rather than at my reflection, moist and giving in the glass. In real-life I am quick and lean, but in the bathroom brushing teeth I become suddenly passive, my center shifts from belly-button to brown-nipple, and I wish my hair Godspeed.

I dredge from the billowing skin of my mouth an intimate taste like reprieve. Like flesh: familiar and no-nonsense. A capsulated sigh. It's sort of like nostalgia, but for something I still have, or am.

Like tonight. Tonight I had so much to clean out of my mouth – weed, kisses, curry, cum, cigarettes, and oranges. A boy with bad skin and a spike through his septum was rolling a spliff in my bed. We took the long way home and he gave me his jacket, black fabric made heavier by the smoky b.o. and inevitable ocean-shaped blotches of beer. We marched through the dense woods, collecting dirt and calling out. He called out to me still, practicing my name in the supposed privacy of flowered sheets (pink background strewn with red). We were both students of obscurity, and sluts on top of that: tacky and jacked-up on hope. I'd gathered so much since the sun simmered down. In two public restrooms, I'd had my moment: bent-double with love in an under-aged club, and later slowed to a halt by implacable shame in the dingy barely-lit gas station bathroom.

It had been a busy day, a day full as a placid face that I would shortly come to hate. I should have been the last thing I could taste right then. And yet as I brushed there it was, swelling up from the back of my throat like a nickname, soft and stern and tragic. A balloon blown from the inside-out. A secret left for too long on the countertop. You can call me Catalina. The unholy amber of the horse's eye. My parents got it wrong.

*

It's cool, it's fresh, it's arresting and real. It's slightly world-weary but also shamelessly innocent, like a young child. It's honest but it doesn't state things tastelessly. If we can get away with that first sentence...

Olivia Scheyer
North Shore Country Day, Winnetka, IL

Dreamland Askew

This morning I sat up
in bed and thought about my
nightly dream of
morning espresso and
a cloudless sky, the only thing
that's unchangeable, always there.
And I looked at my
drooling husband
and my dog at the foot of the bed,
and he looked
at me, sitting up,
from his permanent indentation
on the comforter,
and we glanced at
the splintering wooden floors and
the desk stacked with papers
and we looked at each other
with frustration.
Because all I wanted
for this room, this
extension of my mind,
was a tilt, a bit of
lopsidedness,
so that when I dreamed,
I could place my cup of frothy
espresso on the desk
and suddenly there would be
a drama.

Olivia Scheyer

So that my husband
would roll off the bed and
thud, and the turrets of paper on my desk
would fall into
chaos beside it.
And when my head
started hurting from being
tipped for too long,
I could return to my dream
and drink a deep
breath from that cloudless sky,
not wasting a single molecule, knowing that
the moment I wanted it to,
my breath of sky would
dry up the spilled espresso
and reshuffle my papers and
pick up my husband.

*

Why does the tilt of her room matter? Because without imperfection, you cannot have redemption, that "deep breath from a cloudless sky." The poem's like a little celebration of the bizarre way our heads process what we feel.

Maggy Liu
Saratoga High School, Saratoga, CA

The Story

Twenty minutes before the doorbell rang, my mother ushered us into her bedroom to review The Story.

We sat together on the bed, cross-legged, in our pajamas. On good days, my mother appeared to be aging with grace, the sort of woman who knew how to pair outfit colors and wear makeup appropriately.

Today was not a good day. The yellow light darkened the bags under my mother's eyes, and, if I stared hard enough, I could see the thread-thin veins spider-webbing their way around her eyeballs, feeding her vitamins and blood and sight. With the tired slump of her shoulders and the deep hollows of her neck, she was less than a memory of her normal self.

"Please," she said when she caught me staring, surprisingly calm. "Pay attention. He'll be here any minute." She breathed in, then out through her nose, and began.

"If he asks you if you ever saw Peter hit me, what do you say? Go on," she stuck her chin out at my sister, prompting her.

"He hit you once, and you fell down." My sister Julia was small for her age, and seeing her eyes so serious made me want to sweep her into the minivan and take her to California's Great America, where we could ride The Vortex over and over until the funnel cakes sloshed in our stomachs and the earth was the sky and Peter was just a misguided math tutor who had a crush on Mom. Never mind that I didn't have a license and couldn't tell the brake from the gas pedal – I'd always been good at learning on the fly.

"And where were you when that happened?" She glanced at the alarm clock on the dresser, counting the minutes left.

"In the doorway to the kitchen. You fell down in front of the sink."

My mother had lain there, propped up on her cashmere-clad elbows, unguarded in her disgust. "Only a weak man uses his fists when words would do," she'd always warned me, ever since I let it slip that girls in my grade were starting to go to movies with boys.

"And then?"

"And then I said, 'Are you okay?' and you said, 'I'm fine, go get your sister.'" Julia's tone was nervous but controlled, like a student in the third grade spelling bee. But my lips, not hers, cupped around the letters: D, I, V, O, R, C, E.

She turned to me again, "Please, focus. And where were you during this?"

"I was in my room, sleeping."

I wasn't. I was awake but I didn't want to get up because I was sick of screaming tirades, of accusations, of Peter picking on me for my inability to remember that four times pi times the radius squared equaled the surface area of a sphere. He, too, could calculate the surface of a family perfectly, smiling, "We're fine, and you?" and casually dropping hints about his intimacy with his step-children – "the older one loves grapefruit, so I bought her a bag of them from Costco. The kids just adore me."

I did like grapefruit, but sucking that sour pink flesh in front of his smug and bespectacled face made me sick. He watched as I ate the fruit quietly. At grapefruit number four, I'd gotten up to wash my hands and clean up.

"Won't you eat some more?" He trapped me with gaze, and I stood there, helpless. I couldn't drag that two-letter word out of my lungs, that tiny little word.

I sat back down.

After I'd finished all the fruit that he'd bought me, I left his smirking face and stepped into the dark backyard. There were no stars, but under the moonlight I stepped behind our gardenias and retched everything out. All eight of those round, sunset-colored fruits.

"Did you see anything that morning?"

"No." When I had finally plodded into the kitchen for a bagel, my mother, dressed primly in a skirt and hosiery, had simply ushered me out the door into the waiting car. Her cheek was blood-red, but I'd closed my eyes to it; I would not, could not, deal with that. Cowardice blinded me to her pain.

"And then what happened?" My mother led us through that day, step by step, and I relived it all.

"We went to church. You dropped us off."

"And did I go in?"

"Yes."

"Yes," she repeated, and for the first time that evening, I saw her resolve trip and stumble. She saw in her memory, as I did, the gossiping ladies, the disapproving elders, whispering behind open Bibles. Shame, shame, their voices whispered, until it became a roar echoing in the high-ceilinged congregation chamber.

I saw Mrs. Wellard, the priest's wife, lead her by the elbow into an empty room. With clasped hands and a strung voice, she grabbed my mother. "Oh, sister. You can't leave your husband. Don't be so selfish, please. Your marriage was forged before the eyes of God and you can't destroy that."

And as my mother wrenched her hands free and click-clacked her way out in her heels, Mrs. Wellard cried out, "But think of your children!"

I am.

I can almost hear my mother whispering those words as she stomped across the hall, over the threshold, and into the sun.

"And did he ever hit any of you?" Her frayed voice brought me back to the dimly-lit bedroom.

There was a short pause. My mother glanced at me, then Julia, waiting.

"You have to tell him," she finally said, pinning my sister with her fears and hopes and prayers. Julia's eyes grew and ate up her face. She's only in fourth grade, I wanted to say. Leave her out of this. But I stayed quiet.

"Do you want to have him stay here, in this country? Or worse, stay in this very city? Do you know what he could do? He could drive here when I'm not home and take you both and you'll never see me again."

My sister's ribcage reminds me of slender fingers that curl tightly around some precious treasure, some beautiful heart. It sinks and expands deeply as she squeaks out,

"He slapped me once. When we were on summer vacation."

"And this was at Disney World?"

"Yes."

Can you imagine, in one of those fancy Disney hotel suites with the plush towels and soft bedspreads, with Mickey and the princesses right outside the window and sugar candies and spinning teacups and worlds where children can run to and disappear in when all goes wrong? Where divorce papers are secretly drawn up? Where lovers degenerate into snarling animals, biting and lunging for every last possession? Where family and dreams fall apart as quickly as they're knit together?

Julia had been going on about Aladdin's autograph. "Aladdin is the best!" she screamed over and over while jumping on the luxurious hotel carpet, his signature clutched in her hand.

"Shut up," Peter said, his voice even. I looked up from my book, sensing calamity. I retreated into my corner with my book, the way a bird would disappear before a huge storm.

The way the meek fade before a bully.

When my sister failed to obey, as I knew she would, Peter leaped off the bed, his glasses flashing, and I hid my face so I wouldn't see her tears, her fear. But I still heard her jubilation turn into a primitive howl of terror. I still heard the crack of skin against skin that echoed in between my ears.

After he stormed out of the hotel room, I looked up. Julia sat on the floor, curled up and sniffing, one hand to her burning temple. My little sister met my stare.

Guilt burns more than a slap.

"He ripped it," she finally whispered. I threw down my book and stepped over the "Alad" scrap to hug her.

"I've got some tape," I muttered, but we both knew that tape wouldn't fix anything.

"He never hit you, though. Right?" My mother fixes me with her stare now.

"No." And I suspect, with the sour taste of grapefruit in the back of my mouth, that it's because he and I are alike. Square glasses, the same hunched, monkey-like posture when typing at the keyboard. Both cursed (or blessed) with the preference of books over people.

Both too scared to do the right thing. Both paralyzed by the very idea of confronting people the correct way; instead, we choose fists or frigid silence.

The three of us sit, a triangle bound by the iron-clad strings of love.

The doorbell sounds. The officer steps through the open door, accepts my mother's welcome, and sits Julia and me down at the kitchen table, while my mother sits nervously in a corner.

He produced his badge. "I just need to ask you young ladies some questions." He looked at my mother's ruler-straight spine. "I'll have to ask you to leave the room, ma'am."

"Of course." My mom got up slowly, accepting that this is one fight she can't save us from, only train us for. And I knew then that the only thing that hurts more than the humiliation of a husband's slap is the knowledge that your children will grow up knowing the sound of shame and hate the way that painters know the subtleties of every shade of blue. My mother swept by us with a glance – part scared, part hopeful, but wholly loving – before stepping away to her bedroom.

And I knew that this time, I would not stay silent. I would not close my eyes and bite my tongue about what had happened to my family. All my hurt and anger bundled into my mouth, waiting.

"Right then." The policeman flips open a notepad. "Let's get started."

❋

> *The structure is strong, the character development is powerful. By the end of the story, the mother and her children have this quality about them – it's hard to concretize, but I'll just call it tender humanity – that makes the story frighteningly and lovingly real.*

Kevin Emery
Fine Arts Center in Greenville, SC.

American Soft Drink

after Gwendolyn Brooks

Coke is bubbly and gay. A
joyous endeavor of smiling mannequins, pretty-faced
and laughing. A thing
from the 50's idyllic imps of children. The
drink of crazy straws and white people, a caramel tint.
The cans are red and white, missing a color. Of
necessity we are often pulled
away, but the mushroom clouds are taffy.

✱

At a first reading you might think, "It's nice, but it's about soda." Read it again. There's something very intriguing about the irony in the relation drawn between Coke and Emmett Till. "Of/ necessity we are often pulled/ away, but the mushroom clouds are taffy." Clearly, there is more here than soda.

Jordan Kincaid
Clarkston High School, Clarkston, MI

For Once Will You Respect Me?

You dismiss me
with a "whatever" as I
rage and sputter.
I never needed anything from you,
and had the lowest expectations:
never to take my toothbrush.
Yet your eyeballs roll around
in their sockets, squeezing
drops of disdain from the word
like water from a
dirty dishrag.

I dare them to do that again,
because human eyes
can't take too much
before they twist, torque,
turn bloodshot, then break.
I'll smirk while you shriek
and blood pours from your face,
giggling as your mud-colored
eyes drop from their sockets,
knock against the concrete, travel
down the gravel drive and take
a dive down the storm drain,
where spongy and
pebble-coated they will float.

Jordan Kincaid

I'll gloat over you sprawled on the floor,
digging your fingernails into the carpet
and wailing out cupfuls of scarlet tears –
oh, juicy justice –

but you shove past me
and storm childishly into your room.

*

> It's a punch to the gut, a wash of deliciously vindictive emotions. It's vibrant, strong, salty entertainment poetry, and it goes absolutely for broke. So it's a little gory – but let's face it, frustration can trigger the most explosive recesses of our imagination, and it's a good thing for us to expose that in writing.

Gabriella Gonzales
Bard High School Early College, Manhattan, NY

Parade Ground

My Lazarus emerged
from the peach-ripe

flesh of July dusks
in an instant.

A debutante descent;
what a shock

for two to be united
by the omniscient statuehead.

Red brick, stand witness
to my old lost love. And if

the upper thigh seems
familiar: it is,

and when exposed,
and when like pheromones,

attracted twenty spectres
in a row; black,

and trailed my aching pulse
Home.

Perhaps it's because this poem mentioned Lazarus, but it totally reminds me of a Sylvia Plath poem. It's was mesmerizing and nostalgic and sad, like a trampled parade ground.

Henry Anker
Davis Senior High School, Davis, CA

California Railroad Escape

Seems like a personality passed
since the dusty California day in August
when we walked like Charlie Chaplin
along the ghostly train track machinery,
singing schmaltz in sarcastic harmony
with spirit that swayed the eucalyptus trees.

Talking-talking-talking about our future,
you like it was the last great ball game,
and me like it was a shy girl
painted on the wet plaster wall
of a sinking Venetian chapel.

Two men stood on the tracks above us,
sweating and staring into the sun,
the tall one in a baggy black sweatshirt with the hood hiding his eyes,
and the short one with a beat brown bag of sunflower seeds
sticking out of his pocket like a nagging contradiction.

They asked us for a joint and a light.
I had three broken matches in my shoe
and a cigarette butt I had found three weeks earlier
burning on the floor of Seven Eleven,
as filthy and pitiful as a sparrow with a broken wing.

We each kissed the filter three times but never inhaled,
and the small man flicked it away like an afterthought
while the tall one picked up a pebble and tossed it
at the dying train car parked in the shadow of the freeway.

Train goes to Sa-li-naaas, he said. It don't stop,
And Salinas sounded like a beautiful edge of the world,
and his music sang from headphones threaded through sweatshirt sleeves,
a hip-hop mantra of you won't get far if you stay where you are
you won't get far if you stay where you are.

For a week I lost myself in the abstract
dingy dream of train track spider webs
that whispered escape,
while you disappeared –

to Salinas? to sing songs at the edge of the world?
Or even further to smoke butts with Gandhi
and muse with your dead revolutionary heroes?

Now I've got only boxcar memories of your voice
and the bitter belief that nothing lasts
except for those indifferent towers, those woeful eucalyptus trees,
and my dusty August afternoons.

✷

I'd push for this one. The occasion of this poem, loss, is the occasion for countless bad poems. Steering it away from cliché takes a poet who knows how to bury a kiss in a poem.

Anthony Otten

Lloyd Memorial High School, Erlanger, KY

Felicity Burning

The old man had told him what an accident looked like on a rain-slicked highway: the car, its doppelganger reflected on the muddled mirror of the asphalt, churning like a fiery mattress over the place where reality becomes image. The boy had forgotten to ask him how he'd learned such sacrilegious details.

The boy heard the laughter of pills in the bathroom and didn't like it. He knew it well himself, the turtle-shell smoothness on the fingertip, the delicate impact of hollow body on body.

When the old man emerged, he was waiting for him.

"Dad," he said.

An uncertain smile from the other.

The boy who was hardly a boy anymore leaned on the banister, watching as the man who wasn't terribly old passed. They were close. "What?" the old man asked.

A headshake. "Nothing."

The old man tried to nudge around him. The son stood with his arms akimbo. "What's this?" the old man asked.

"I heard a rattle."

"I ain't a car. I can rattle and be just fine."

The boy reached.

The old man twisted away like a lynx and broke past him. Something chattered in his pocket. "What's that?" the boy said.

"Lawd a mercy," the old man said in his downward, wine-breathy way, and stalked down the staircase with a parched laugh, slightly unsteady. The door opened below and a fringe of cool came to his son's cheek, a breeze that could've been imagination touching him. The open plain of possibilities laid bare. Or maybe this was just how he always remembered that moment the door shut, its impact on the jamb rattling in his marrow. Outside an engine chuffed awake, viciously alive.

❋

> There's something so striking about this writer's facility with language. Attention all you young writers out there: if you want to do something in less than three hundred words, your words should twist, churn, and chuff. They should be like people, like engines, like animals.

Jane Ligon

Lewis and Clark High School, Spokane, WA

Colorado

There was road, there was sun, there was heat, and the car. He'd been driving for hours, the time ticking by with the radio. All that existed was asphalt and paint, guiding him, carrying him through hills and valleys and fields, the dizzy sky. He didn't see the bird until it was upon him, hitting the windshield, head bobbing on the wipers, watching until he pulled over, the body lost miles back. He took the bird's head and buried it in the dry dirt on the edge of a gas station, marked the grave with a pen, said it was a good bird. Then he drove away, cleaning the windshield as he went.

It's snappy, poignant, and just creepy enough. It seeks to answer one of the toughest questions – how do we react when grief/death is literally thrust upon us? And what is our responsibility? It does a great job in answering as much as it can in just 113 words.

Tom Costello
Hastings High School, Hastings, NY

Platonic Rigidity

Back straight, straight, we can
be beautiful together. What are
the sociological ramifications
of teenagers who drink amnesia
in deserted parks? I chewed sidewalk
for you. I tell people my acne
is sunspots.

I stand with crooked vertebrae
and think (stars are track marks,
freckles on the back of
my neck) of everything but how
the sun bends me like
a shadowpuppet, and I am
trapped in this shifting cave of a person
and I fell in love with
a streetlight because it
didn't love me back and
I want to itch my skin off
sometimes, because depression is
a kind of fire too. But all I do is
pick these chunks of gravel
out of my mouth and
fling them at moonbeams,
and ride the subway because
I love to shake, I want to hollow
out my cheeks and stuff them
with everything, everything, everything.

This one literally gave me chills. It's raw and ugly and beautiful all together. I like how it's blatant; its beauty is that it's so honest.

Rooftop

Hands dusted of peach pits,
Gravel, and feathered things
Which perch in souls,

Tiptoes clutching the ledge,
Rawboned, everything within us
Groping for the courage to leap.

Pulses jagged. Vertigo.
A fraying tidbit of time –
All we ever wanted was to fall.

You examined the sprawl below,
The wrinkled visage of landscape and fractal cities,
Watched people pursue the horizon
And declared the world flat.

I remember looking at my toes for a long time.

You didn't laugh when I asked you,
But you didn't say yes.

We walked back home.

✸

What's most impressive is that the style and approach of the piece is constantly evolving, constantly adapting to a new perspective. Without our noticing it goes from bright and pounding and impatient, whirring along through detached phrases and intense emotions, to an almost excruciating, ponderous set of statements dripping in depth and weight.

Jules Ray
The Fine Arts Center in Greenville, SC

In Which I Postulate

after Gwendolyn Brooks

With my sister I
kvetch about love and need and want.
What does that mean? Is it the same as a

man in a bathroom taking a peek
or a woman standing at
the corner of 10th and 35th where the
Greeks own a diner – in the back

they argue with the other Greeks about where
the best gyros are (hint: it's
at Stavros' across the bridge in the rough
part of Queens) – and

is it the same as Harlem kids running untended
banging on doors with their black-and-blue fists and
nudging at the exposed ribs of the hungry

homeless. The teens are rolling weed
stolen from the empty lot where it just grows,
sneering at a passing tourist or a cop or a
balloon-bellied girl

who, because her boy left her, gets
money for when the small-child is sick
from the government, of
the government and is it the same as a

woman begging for a rose?

It's a little rough at the edges in a good way. It's somehow playful and earnest and hopeful. There's something essentially adolescent about the voice that I like, at that moment where you begin poking at the world and realizing you can't figure things out, but you might as well try.

Searching Through the Lost and Found at the 21st Street Pool Hall

after Kenneth Koch

When I lost my tolerance for desire,
I couldn't find a way for –
(whom? for you? for fame?) –

for a chance to find a loss and
a way to find a love –
for ratty gloves and batteries – and

all I needed was to find anonymity
in a world of lost watches and found dogs, and
I am completely full

of the lost ideas with which my mind is fledged –
with ideologies of Schrodinger, loss and Communism,
even though a cat and a button and a mark attracted

the masses to it, through me
and from me. We sifted through the box of coats and glasses to
connect the lost to the found to the you.

The themes of love and fame and masquerade work beautifully for me. I want to have written those last two lines myself.

Maia Silber

Hendrick Hudson High School, Montrose, NY

Visiting Day

    Three hours on the train to visit great-aunt in Providence for her 96th birthday. We sit at a hard plastic table with cheesy rose designs and dust settled in its cracks. She looks at me and I look at her and I think that she's got some lipstick on her teeth but not any on her lips. She looks at me and I look at her and she thinks that I am wearing a lot of eyeliner for a Young Person. I swirl the ice in my glass so it clinks on the sides. My hands get restless and the ice gets loud but great-aunt doesn't notice because her hearing-aids are broken again. She asks me would I like something to eat and I say no because I had a muffin on the train and also because she gets her food from that deli with the broken sign and it's always gone bad. We don't talk after that so I swirl my ice some more. Time squeezes by like the last drops of ketchup from a bottle and after a while she asks how am I enjoying tennis lessons and I say very much even though I don't play tennis; that's my cousin James. I glance at her cheaply-made wooden clock and notice it has been two hours and it's time to leave for soccer practice and maybe see a movie later. She gives me a kiss on the cheek which feels like getting poked with a toothbrush and I hope she doesn't get any orangey lipstick on me. I say happy birthday.

✱

Been there. The whole thing is just strangely, nicely comical. Commas make too much sense for these moments in life you have to squeeze for their poetry.

Anran Yu
Desert Vista High School, Phoenix, AZ

Heartprison

i tried to lock you away
in a prison of ribs
with lungs for company and
a spine for a trembling warden,
but you crept up my throat
and rearranged the lies on my tongue
so others could see you more clearly.

i tied the knots in my hair
into a cradle, and dyed it black
so you would sleep,
but you became the ocean and
drowned my senses until
i washed out the night and
allowed your tides to carry away
my pessimistic thoughts.

finally i held you down,
clipped your wings,
and pressed you between
the pages of a journal,
but your inkblood made its home
in the lines of my palms
and your bird-light bones
cracked under each step i took.

that winter i buried you deep
and hoped that the frozen ground
would teach you to be cold and hard,
but when spring rose with the lakes
i watched you plunge into the sky –

(and it occurred to me then
that perhaps i was the one
locked away all along
and you, dear heart,
you were the dove
outside my window
whose destination i could
never quite make out.)

✱

The poem is beautiful. A great example of how a writer's power over words expresses the futility of the speaker's attempts. I was blown away by the quiet love and revelation encapsulated so simply. The sheer honesty with which Anran expresses love is wonderful.

Gabe Lunn
Saint Michael's University School, Victoria, BC

Bury Me with a Shot of Espresso

Here on the rim,
my lip print sits in blurred lines
on an earthenware mug, dark with black tea
the barista recommended.
Elderlies fill the chain café,
sipping number 3s and 5s,
awaiting their turn for the microphone's grace
to rearrange
the words of their children's postcards
into a round of applause.
In the city,
nobody from your block
really knows where the number nine bus takes you.
You're just a prop in the frame in their 8mm camera.
In the corner of this steaming and sipping café,
in the cushions of an IKEA chair,
I am nothing more than a lens, capturing
the shifts of their lips and cheeks.
A goateed man stands and tells us,
"This is an exercise where we write our last words:
Don't shoot. Thank you."
This is what it must feel like
to be in outer space,
an awkward sense of the inappropriate.

I love the mood of this poem, and how the character notices not only actions but the traces left behind- the lip prints, the shifting of faces. It reads seamlessly, each line in holistic harmony with the other. The poem acquires a distinct personality, a tone that asks for low lighting, slouched posture, and quiet contemplation.

Rebecca Greenberg
Wheeler School, Providence, RI

The Christening

We decided not to make mud pies.

Our stout little fingers were already connoisseurs of that field of culinary art. We knew how much water to add to make the mixture malleable but not too watery; we knew how to roll the mud-balls in our fingers, between the palms of our hands to achieve a perfect spherical shape. We knew the limits of the shovel's power, and when to use our nails to pry the rocks ensconced in the walls of an incipient hole. We knew that digging for the smoothest, moistest dirt beneath the chapped super-stratum required patience, and knew that our hands would resurface with reverse French-manicures and brown stains. We knew worms and did not fear them. We would pick their gummy bodies as though they were clover blossoms, move them elsewhere and keep digging. They were good to the earth – we had seen the evidence: their swirling spirals of dirt sprouting from the soil like tiny castles. Centipedes, however, we would hew in two with the shovel, finding no excuse to let their repulsive bodies cross ways with us with impunity.

Today our fingers read the earth with solemnity.

We scoured the earth methodically, following an unwritten recipe. Our hands transmitted well the higher, more dignified purpose held in our minds. Mud pies were like crayons to the ebony pencil; we had simply outgrown them.

Today we kept our nails clean – not just to remain unsoiled for the incoming ceremony, but because we used the pads of our fingers, not our prying nails, to smooth out what was formerly a crude, angular hole into a polished basin.

Before us, her entire body carefully contained within a broad Norway maple leaf, her bleached polyester hair coruscating in the sun, sat Kelly in her silken princess gown. Her eyes were a beautiful, solid aqua or turquoise, which we had both claimed to be our favorite color and yet had failed to find anywhere but on nail polish or fancy '60s cars. A blue that was too still, a blue that reflected nothing at all, only stared in a garish magnificence at a point we could never quite locate despite the constant tilting of our heads to follow her gaze. Her mouth remained disclosed at all times, flaunting a toothpaste smile.

Cybèle reached out and took Kelly, who still smelled like newly molded plastic, like the box from which she had emerged this morning. My sister twirled a finger through the lustrous fluidity of her hair. Like the mouth, it was frozen, for no matter how long Cybèle twisted her hair it would always right itself, resume its stick-straight position down her back, static and waveless as before. Cybèle did this a few times more, the platinum waterfall reiterating its stubborn lifelessness every time.

The doll was laughing at us. But we both smiled. The scissors were restless as a captured grasshopper in her hands. The silver beak caught the light once, then shot through Kelly's hair. The white-gold tufts fell noiselessly beneath, indolent as snowflakes, ignorant of the destruction around them. On the lawn, the locks still bunched dense and fresh like miniature bouquets of roses. In a joyful rage we scattered the residues of Kelly's locks, flicking and disarranging the pile till some lost their dreamlike whiteness in the dust and others took off, carried by the breeze in lazy marbled wisps.

We stared a moment at our profanity, like new criminals shocked at the blood they shed. But the blades in our hands did not sleep for long. The scissors became wolves' jaws, tearing at the silk.

And then Kelly's shorn head looked up, still filled with mirth, her feet hidden in a patch of snow. Now the maple leaf beneath her seemed as unnecessary as the satin gown and and we let her bare body lay before the sun. Her cropped head collected smut and turned dusky white like a soiled cotton ball.

Her smile was defiant now, reckless.

I poured the water in the basin, and we watched the water suck the dirt greedily and become brown. Cybèle picked up Kelly and pressed her little foot into the side of our font. The imprint of her foot was toeless, archless, a rectangle – prosaic like the imprint of a penny.

Kelly's foot was dirty now. My sister placed the little imp waist deep, pushing hard till her feet squelched in the mud below. And then we cupped the water and poured it over her head.

We held our breath. Her skin was as candy-pink as ever. We renounced the solemn ritual.

We plunged her in head-first, rolling her body in the slough, raked her head against the walls of the font, until any trace of whiteness in her hair was gone. This satanic immersion done, we picked her up to examine her – between her lips a brown strip replaced the white and she was a brunette, dirtier than our dirty blond. But the brackish water would not permeate her glossy surface, collecting instead in brown beads over her arms and stomach. We poured mud in lieu of water over her head, watching the motes of dirt stay nestled in the crooks of her eyes, and above her cheekbones. We ripped more dirt from the font and rubbed her skin with the stinking chrism, the thin film of dirt coating her body till her skin turned a sulphurous brown.

We modeled a huge ball of mud, its formless contents oozing and flowing in dark streams down our arms, and sank Kelly's body in its depths. Solemn bishops no more, we were whimsy gods now, and could do as we pleased. We carved the body from the mud itself, and watched the sphere dwindle to a vaguely star-like shape until her arms and legs protruded and gradually her whole body exposed itself again. We placed our ugly Eve facing the sun; and exposing her dirty, naked, and torn, we forced feeling into that plastic cage.

"She can't be called Kelly anymore," my sister said, watching the mud cake on her head.

And we did not – at least in principle. We called her Adèle, Maya, Flora, anything but Kelly, but every time we saw her that name flopped out from our mouths despite ourselves. Our little human irrevocably bore the same name as the plastic princess before her and those blue eyes still stared, unabated in their artificial fury.

✱

I feel like this is what literary nonfiction should be. It has a greater meaning but isn't shoving it down your throat. It reads fluidly and has wonderful craft. It tells of a wonderful sisterly relationship but also delves into our relationship with the inanimate objects of the world.

Kathleen Maris
Fine Arts Center, Greenville, SC

Winter

after Charles Simic

In Winter, we wandered through blizzards, with
coats left behind, dresses cut short. My
face reddened in a cold blush from my heart,
and my hands ached, as if icicles had grown and spiked
within them. But their hands had turned blue and
chapped, creases cut and spilled, bleeding,
and I said nothing. Snowdrifts gathered on
our shoulders, pressed the tree to tug its
visitors in with clawed branches.

✳

This piece has the soul of two poems, coming from both Charles Simic's haunting line punctuating the piece and the edge of winter that the author so deftly conveys. It takes the Golden Shovel format and runs with it, creating a tone that is as beautiful as it is nostalgic. It screams inspiration.

Jack Nachmanovitch

Charlottesville High School, Charlottesville, VA

300 Dead Blackbirds

1.
Lying in the snow, like bits of charcoal –
I can't help but think of the Wind
smearing them around
with her thumb
        as if she were only trying to draw herself,
a charcoal portrait in the disappearing snow.

2.
A washing machine crumpling around black socks,
like a cloud of birds –
        we wait for them
to come out the other
end, all clean and smelling crisp
        as if we, too, could be new
again.
    Because how could we hit the ground
so hard it opens up our bodies,
fills our mouths with snow and highway?

3. Maybe the birds just decided
they didn't want to be alive anymore, like when ancient trees,
        white-washed bones of the earth,
simply fall over. Maybe the birds just dropped out of the sky.
It must have been beautiful.

Plummeting, they probably looked like fighter jets
with their wings, the helplessly flapping smoke.
They hit the snow, like water mixing with water,
an alchemy of boundaries.

❋

The swirling ideas of vulnerability and questioning and, well, dead birds, remind me a little bit of P. Hurshell's "In Winter," one of my favorite poems of all time.

Hayun Cho
North Shore Country Day, Winnetka, IL

Flight

When an uncle dies
does the sky shake and
do mothers and sisters
suddenly stop
do babies
the little nieces
clutch his toy train and
break it
blue and spilling
down the middle

thunderbolt in a clear sky
that was the prophecy
my grandfather heard
from the shaman
and it happened in June
uncle was driving up
a mountain road and then
broken bones
scattered in red young
space like charms
space that beat sadly like
old drums

the rooms screamed
and my grandmother fell
my grandfather sang arirang
the mourning song
that has all the achings of failing light

the closeness of the dead
like a true Korean
and they bounced off darkness
like a mirror

my mother held my hand
as his ghost snapped at
our elbows and knees
already cold and hoping
for perhaps a familiar touch

this perpetual boy
leaving
who wrote love letters
and drank milk continuously
he bought my mother
fried chicken
trapped fowl
the panic and joy of flight
into the peppery flakes
for her growing belly
perhaps then I began to kick
the yellow oil and
blood and sky
cradling my dawn-light limbs
perhaps they called my name

oh this forever boy
he haunted her
and now I hear voices

Hayun Cho

boy boy almost man
he taught me the mechanics of flight
air palm air blue blue blue
the loveless dip and
rush of landing.

�֍

This piece shares with us the fragile nature of the human condition, and it does so by adopting a voice of quiet power. It resembles a piece of music; the crescendos and decrescendos, the invisible stop signs at the end of each line that ask us to pause, to rest, to take in an image before we move on to appreciate the next one. Subtle yet evocative, cautious but generous, it's a keeper, to be sure.

Ghost Song

I write him
I envision black eyes
a soft mouth
maybe even my mother's
cheekbones light and tracing
I grip the crayons
and somehow I know
there will be a ghost soon
smoothing the crooked page
my absent uncle
hollow blue space
wet soft stone uncle
the kind that smiles and
disappears into oceans
submerging our half mute lives
mid song

we are like birds
living restless in this space
smelling of cheese and rice
milk and soybean soup
sometimes the dead linger
all half mouths and long hair
like old mothers
hungry for the love of their own
children

so I dare uncle's sea
to come here and tell me
who we are
to find the little girl and perhaps
fashion her wings of
oil and ashes
instead he kisses my cheek

before the long flight back
through forests of flowers that smell
of family blood and rain
through the mountain graves
and muddy bones claiming
the markers and earth that lie
sad and torn from the summer storms

he might have split the sky in half
just for me and let the dawn come early
just enough uneasy horizon
that pulses under the damaged clouds
and smells of newness and
leftover regret

that night
we remembered each other
in the morning
I kick aside the mattress
stories rattling like coughs
impatient in my chest
old songs in my mouth and
arms full of sea water
I run the voices under my tongue
like pebbles in his pyre
and they are blue
like air like
flying sound

This poem is poignant without feeling melodramatic, simplistic without feeling underwritten, and fluid without feeling uncontrolled; a combination that's hard to come by. The author successfully avoids trying too hard to make the ghost song 'haunting' – it could've easily become a tragedy, but there's just enough fragile beauty within the imagery to balance it out.

Katia Diamond
Westwood High School, Mesa, AZ

Come Sunday

when winter traps and breaks
it is always a rebirth,
a resurrection, a stretching newborn.

heaviness.
it was 3:33
detours through mumblings and slips
of wet worm tongues
all the breathing of battle-broken bells
and digital clocks blinking in the semi-dark.
weary walking, the sinking of coins into fountain water,
cursing my pewter tongue, tip-toes.

coming into my own kind of bravery – to watch the lifting-up
of a sweet pink mouth, the shy peaking of teeth,
the darkening, kindling of titian eyes.

hear roughness of voice, catch and turn of tone,
and allow myself to re-descend, and again.
finally, silence the hoarse, dead voice in my mind which prophesies
her bruises, the wounding of someone too precious;
one person i could not bear to damage.

365: nothing, the banging rhythm
of double entendres –
365: nothing,
white backs and the quick thieving of special sights,
then back i slink to stunted dreaming.
finally, 365: what? we tear down the damn wall,
the touch of finger-shoulder; suddenly
11:11 wishes are tossed back, fountain water, pennies

whimper. they're nothing to me.
finger-lip, whisper-cheek, eye to eye.
voice is gone, winter: done, and now my breath is halted
as i know how lucky i am.

i will treasure this feeling
of drumming, moving togetherness.

There's a beating pulse to this thing with its fast-paced narration, alternating between letter and number. Although the imagery is disjointed, the lack of cohesion is forgiven because the imagery is presented to the reader through the same lens — quick clipped semi-metaphorical images that at once thrive in the physical world and depart from it altogether.

Upasna Saha

Hunter College High School New York City, NY

Even You Can't See the Universe, Sweetheart

I asked you for freedom and you asked me for answers.

I said there was no logical reason to throw myself off an airplane with nothing but a parachute, but I wasn't conceived logically. (Never underestimate the power of spiked punch and a fraternity boy or a high school valedictorian with a full scholarship.) Logically, my biological parents shouldn't have had me, let alone raised me themselves. I'm just keeping tradition.

You stared at me over your book with the hands that had rubbed my tears when I had tried my first (and last) cigarette. You said you had no idea what I was saying.

So I tried again, folding my legs on the chair that still had a sauce stain from last night's spaghetti and meatballs. It's too difficult for me not to slurp the noodles. I reminded you that after yesterday's dinner, ringing with the perfect amount of salt (an operation you alone had commandeered), we'd ignored the stack of DVDs and collapsed on the bed.

You promised me a late night movie marathon whenever I wanted.

I groaned and that made you set your book down and switch your full attention from astrophysics/quantum mechanics/biomechanical engineering to me, because as a rule, I do not lose my composure. Not ever and not now. I said no, that wasn't it, science could never explain it, and all artists had tried, oh they tried, but all they ever got was really horseshoe close, and that's as close as anyone would ever get, because we're human. That's how it's meant to be.

There was a faint spark in your eyes but your voice was measured when you said you still couldn't see how this it mattered.

I told you yes, it matters to everything, because no us would have ever existed without an it, because it is the common denominator in everything that anybody has ever done. Do you think that Albert Einstein's theory of relativity just popped into his head one day while he was talking a leisurely stroll around his garden? Do you think Pablo Picasso just picked up a blue paintbrush and forgot to paint in any other color for a couple of years? Gustave Eiffel didn't happen to dream up his tower, darling, and Emily Dickinson didn't put in dashes only because she thought they were pretty. Now you can explain and I will wait until you explain until your breath gives out and the stars are all dead.

You filled me a glass of water because I felt winded, and you watched as I drank. I know all you wanted was something that would help you understand because love never means you quite get it all, but I promise you, my thirst for water holds no epiphanies for anyone. You exhaled and posed the question I think most of us have grapple with for the majority of our lives.

"Is this what you really want?"

I cupped the glass so tightly that one more slight ounce of pressure, might send shards into my eye and blind me for life. Yet there was nothing else to hold on to if I started to cry.

I said that this house was yours and mine, even if it wasn't ours. There was no way I was moving out, and I wanted you to stay, too, if you could. We could still have that late night movie marathon after dinner, even though you'll still probably be contemplating gene manipulation/multiverse theory/chemical warfare. But that's okay, because no one ever gets it all.

You nodded and picked up your book, and said that you'd get breakfast ready while I took a shower.

This might very well be the closest I'll get to everything.

❋

A story of exquisite moments. There's a quiet pulchritude to it that's endearing and also a bit seductive. Two things really won me over: the narrator's personality – of meticulous temperament, of quiet assertiveness, of composed reservation – and the attention to details that complements her personality and her relationship with the addressee.

Room 201

Now the quarantine. Four white walls
closing in.
Benedictions have become too feeble
to wrestle the wilting of body tissues.
All I hear is the clink of nickels as someone leaves
to light a cigarette.
Now the inertia. Taciturn,
pretending to scrutinize cuticles.

As we listened to him respire under the thin sheets
we knew the steps to take and the arrangements
to make. Forty-five hours later, the ice thawed –
why did we linger by the doorsteps
until the moon peered into the ward?

Love this poet. Her poems are built from pools within pools, moments within moments, with every last line carrying its own universe of unspoken emotions and expectations. She's an absolute genius with negative space.

The Report on Apricots

Then came the time when the final knot
Had to be untangled. When the cobweb
In the corner had to be dusted.
We sat and watched the vast blue,
Opened the small crumpled book
That had lain shut the past two summers.
She unfolded my fist and lay in my palm
A roseate apricot, sweetly scented.
Perhaps leaving the cirrus of a season
That would never come again.
A bundle of cumulus. Snapdragons.
And when I bit into early summer,
April sun spilled down my windowpane.

*

I'm completely in love with it – the flight from gravity, the faint tingle of waiting, the sweet patience, the pulse, the silence, the light tumbling forth from a half-forgotten memory. It's an ode to what we've both forgotten and refused to forget.

Laura Wanamaker

Walnut Hill School for the Arts, Natick, MA

Ovule

The sanctuary's egg as always,
Blue egg, robin's egg, half full
Of gold and embryo,
And what I celebrate, stages.
The cross with Her gaunt giant,
Like a last school portrait;
His passage, the whole album ethical.
I think I've nearly out walked Christ;
He almost owes me something.
I've said His name so many times
I almost bleed His saline.
I've drunk a total keg of blood
Here on this cushioned footrest.

You never liked the Holy part of me,
The wine-drunk, God-scoffed hemisphere
Of me. Dry fingered, upright, wooden,
Uneating, scale-faced, fishy memories
Interrupt "Our Father:"
I left the headlights on to watch you bend,
To see you crouch, for the first time
Lower, to tie your shoe before dinner,
Before we vampires ducked Heaven,
And I kneeled before you last night.
A salty Unholy, full of silver fish when I spit.
I wish I could trick like Lilith – left out
Of the Bible – who curled around a juicy sin.

I wish I were praying for forgiveness,
But I pray for God to reach warmth,
Rip the seam of my belly through button,
And squeeze until I beat my chest
Like I'm sure Judas did, to help him swallow
The kiss. As I'm sure he did as it evolved,
And a spongy, red trunk cracked his jaw apart,
And, rooted to the spot, he couldn't unzip.
I watched you lurch, draped boatside,
Slacker, sticker, break-backer. I supple thump
To bring the seed up. I, too, Judas, try to swallow the kiss,
Kiss this man's salty neck to keep the leaves down.
I, too, don't pray to Christ, but to His ribs.

This poet seems to relish in getting us in the thick of her language, but without the cost of tangential veerings. And the Judas-kiss line was brilliant. I think I actually heard my mind being blown (it sounded a bit like "whichhowwww").

Summer 2011: Images

6/12/11
The house, like a white horse carcass on a hill.

6/13/11
Sister #2, in nothing but tie-dye PJ shorts, stands on the pantry counter before the shelves stuffed with cans, bags, and boxes.

6/14/11
Little brother, exiled to the basement; lies on a black leather barbell bench, orange foam popping from its bindings; lifts a weight thicker than his bicep; his neck holds his head to see over his stomach at the spider-webbed wall; he is older than me, I feel.

6/16/11
Sister #1, beside her best friend, Kylie – the Feminine, the Motherly – dressed like a boy, looks, too. The pride at fooling someone in passing; the armor in those baggy clothes.

6/17/11
The gray hairs – thicker, curlier – boing from my stepmother's hopeful Japanese-style bun.

6/18/11
In the wee hours of the morning, I wake to the sound of someone moving. In the hallway, I meet my father, in only his Grinch boxers, bald and soft as an old man.

6/19/11
Leah puts on her ballet shoes – the way she doesn't use her thumbs as much as most people – and does an arabesque for me, sloppy but real, one from the heart of a girl who will never be a ballerina.

6/20/11
Leah's face relaxes into a dull, slow expression when she sees her face in the mirror. Everyone has a "mirror face." Hers is one of disappointment.

6/21/11
I remember my mother's collarbones. The same as mine, but cut deeper with age. There were miniscule, red veins under her skin that gave her a rich, reddish tint. If I were mire clay, she was Arizona.

6/22/11

Leah, underwater, lit from behind by pool light. Her dark hair turned to purple fog.

6/24/11

Ben Franklin is ankle-deep in cow blood. Or is it the new carpet they put in this past winter?

6/25/11

Some other, big-shot biker on the trail ahead of me, with NISSAN written across his big, red ass.

6/26/11

On the bike trail, a skinny old lady rollerblading, ancient body pumping like a loom.

6/27/11

There it is, the calling card for my mother's death (we gave them out), with her smiling, wise face, perched on my boss's desk: ROBIN GOELLNER 1960-2010. "Nice to see you, too, Barbara. I'm glad to be back."

6/28/11

I saw the pet bunny in a new light, as Sister #1 told me, "Sometimes – and not really, I don't really mean it – I just wish Doodle would die already!" Oh Doodle, the Unheld.

6/29/11

I was afraid of the darkness, parked like a train, between the water shoe shelves and the T-shirts in the store's basement.

6/30/11

Today, I wake to sunlight shining through the window fan, like a beating heart.

7/2/11

Sometimes, I get these looks from people who at least liked my mother from afar. I checked this woman out at the register today – the mother of a boy who used to give me a different kind of look in middle school – and she gave me the Look: eyes got smaller, as if on the verge of smiling, but mouth corners tucked in, and eyebrows slightly tilted out to the sides as if she were taking in a painting.

7/3/11

Jar of water balloons on the lace-draped dining room table, like bloated eyeballs.

7/4/11

Jack leans over the saloon door from behind the register, watching the parade, and I see his arms bent like that – elbows pointing to the ground, T-shirt sleeves pushed up to his shoulders, making a "W" – and his face in ¾ profile, and suddenly his beauty strikes me, and I can't help but picture him in black and white.

7/5/11

This man obviously has never worn sandals before today. Perfectly tanned, like a Ken doll, with muscular thighs, he follows his two young sons from aisle to aisle. He seems a good father, though trapped by his domestic responsibilities (as I assume all married grown-ups on vacation are, dissatisfied with their lives and once-lovers, who don't even look at them anymore when they get out of the shower in the morning), but what a sock tan. From his calf to his toes, he's a deadman's shade of pale.

7/6/11

Bonfires along the sand like scabs.

7/8/11

This morning, I got to watch Twitch take his makeup off. After the whole night on the beach, he was pale and shaking, like the boys I imagine. He used a WetOne, abundant because of his new, baby sister. The sink was a basin glued to the counter with a vintagey spigot, and over it, he wiped off the bottom liner first. Then, with another WetOne, his forehead and cheeks and chin, the cloth turning dusty with foundation. He dropped the used cloths into the basin. With another WetOne, he got the tops of his eyes, the cat eye part, and his hands were shaking; especially his left, which he actually had to steady halfway through, out before him, reflected in the antique mirror as he glanced up to see his half-finished face. I saw myself there, over his shoulder, my own makeup smudged, but nicely, like I'd been having fun.

7/9/11

Today, I cleaned for a woman, and on her window was the most incredible bug. It could have been made from glass, but its thorax wasn't a centimeter long. Like a dragonfly, but with two, long, needle-like tails from its narrow torso. With those, it was almost two inches long.

7/10/11

The clothes on my floor look like the toppings of a vegetarian pizza.

7/11/11

My two little warts – one right on the middle knuckle, the other in the curve between that and the next knuckle – remind me of cauliflower. I believe this means they are common warts, as opposed to plantar.

7/12/11

My stepmother yelled at my brother for putting Sister #2 to bed until he ran out of the house and I ran into my room. Now, he paces the lawn, in his white T-shirt and khaki shorts, so much lighter than the night, so much like the sky with all his freckles, in the tall grass, wading.

7/13/11

Leah's drunk on my floor with her cellphone. I'm on the bed, looking down at her goofy face. She's talking to the boy she loves, in the stilted language of a Boston gangster.

7/15/11

Anger, for me, is a black lotus, heavy on my diaphragm, lazy petals flopping open to reveal the juicy epicenter.

7/17/11

No towels again. I pictured myself from behind, walking down the hall, not dripping, but streaming water onto the hardwood floor, like a mermaid, walking down the long, antique hallway, butt naked.

7/18/11

Harry Potter: The last time the "WB" will mean so much. Behind those smoky logo letters, lie thousands of midnight breaths. The witching hour holds us like swimmers going in.

7/19/11

Sharon wears her gauges well. Today, when she dropped in to see me at work, she wore pink, metal circles inside of the holes in her ears, with yellow lightening bolts through the middles. She's not like the other girls with gauges. She wears them like a medicine woman.

7/20/11

The slow feet-to-head Jack gives me as I walk from the back of the store in my long, tight dress.

7/21/11

Tommy, Tommy, Tommy, the Boy Who Was More Attractive in the Dark. No more acne. His eyes looked lighter, bluer, clearer, bigger. He was stunned by the little stories I had to tell, my head in his lap. I couldn't even tell if there was food in his braces.

7/23/11

This morning, I rode my bike under the telephone wire, and this time, there were two Barbies, their hair melted together, melted to the wire, identical aside from their outfits: one in a half-blue, half-yellow one-piece, and the other in a purple top and pink bottom with lace around the legs.

We sell those Barbies at Ben Franklin.

7/24/11

Jack was hung over today. I watched him stock water shoes slowly. His hair was sticking to his forehead and neck (not that unusual because Jack sweats a lot, but he was sweating more than usual) in commas.

7/25/11

People look nicer when you're drunk. All their blemishes blend into the better parts of their bodies. But they're meaner to you when they know you're drunk. A man at Cumberland Farms, who was a senior when I was in eighth grade, told me to "Get out!" and I was offended. Didn't he remember how beautiful other people looked once?

7/26/11

Warts: The skin around where I'm burning them off is flaking, and I can't help thinking that a white rose is blooming up from my knuckles.

7/27/11

The rest of us watch Franky and Devon out by the water with curiosity. Five years since our favorite story: When Franky reached into Devon's pants one night after a show (they were dating in middle school) and then hastily drew back with, "There's hair down there!" Now, they stand like adults, big college kids, Devon in a tight, black cocktail dress, in red lipstick, and Franky in a suit and tie, which flaps out against his shoulder in the wind. They laugh, and Devon has her hand on his chest for a moment.

7/28/11

The handles of my bike like the horns of a bull under the heels of my hands.

7/29/11

Some people have trouble imagining their grandparents having sex. It was my grandparents' anniversary a little while ago, and I was wondering how they celebrated it. They probably watched CSI and then read and then fell asleep, practically mirrors of each other by now, but I almost want them to have banged and banged hard, like a sack of potatoes and a sack of corn in the back of a farm wagon on the dirt road into town one fine Saturday morning in Kansas.

8/1/11

I made a doodle on the back of a receipt today during one of the slow hours. It was off a stick figure – bauble head, narrow hips – with bangs, holding out a heart that shot off straight spikes of light, on her little, flat, fingerless hands. A series of well-placed dashes showed her blushing. And before her, was a much taller line of a boy with a bauble at the top, and wisps of feathery hair. A small dot made his eye. A curve above made his eyebrow. And a slightly larger circle made his mouth. And then I realized it was Jack and I, and I realized that he wasn't the kind of boy to hold a heavy heart that asked to be taken for a little while. And I also realized why I was so eager to hand it to someone.

8/2/11

More than anything, I don't want to miss this: jumping up and down in flickering or flashing light, unable to feel my face, my arms and my hair making seaweed in the air, and knowing with certainty that I am still young.

8/3/11

Muscles in my calves make grooves so deep I can't help but think of puzzles and pieces and continents and Pangea and coming back together.

8/4/11

My brother and I put our feet together, heel to heel, and the balls of my feet fit into his arches.

8/5/11

The cat, Sophie, asleep with Sister #1 in her bed. Sophie's paws were out in front of her, touching Sister #1's palms, which were also held out. Do they share their dreams, too?

8/6/11

No one breathes fire like Matt does. Bent over the pit, matchbook open in his hand, he breathes with the wind and brings the seaweed to smoke, brings a tangerine glow to his face.

8/7/11

The tourist kids want to run out, into the grass, to the elbow. I remember one evening – when I was younger, before Walnut Hill, when I ran out alone, and on the way back I found a dead wolf, not like a dog at all, but sinewy and black, with a bushy tail, in a deep pit in the sand. I remember feeling like I could have been killed for seeing it – and the memory of really running, scared, back to the parking lot, stops me.

*

> *This is literary nonfiction like I've never seen. It's a gorgeous, frank, and moving mosaic of the human condition; the prose lilts and eddies and swoops through the author's adolescence, reflecting themes of life and death and youth and love. This is all you can ask for in writing, really, and it's pieces like these that make me so grateful to be editing.*

Polyphony H.S. volume VIII

Contributors' Bios

Henry Anker is a member of the graduating class of 2013 at Davis Senior High School in Davis, CA. He has self-published a bilingual book of essays based on his experiences as a teacher in surrounding migrant communities and his fiction has been featured in *The Blue Moon Literary and Art Review*.

Emma Arett lives in St. Louis Missouri and attends Metro Academic and Classical High School. She will graduate in 2013. In 2012, she received the *River Styx* magazine Founders' Award for poetry as well as the first place title in the St. Louis Poetry Center's Hopkins Memorial Poetry Contest. She loves pets, purses, and Diet Coke.

Anna Blech is a student at Hunter College High School in New York City, Class of 2014. She likes to read, act, and sing, and her specialty is writing one-act musical comedies. Her plays, "Parent-Teacher Conference: The Musical" and "College Admissions: The Musical," both received national Scholastic writing awards.

Hayun Cho attends North Shore Country Day School in Winnetka, IL (Class of 2013). She can often be found scratching out a poem, re-reading books, and savoring the excellent chickpea curry at her local Indian restaurant. Hayun aspires to be a poet, novelist, and literature professor someday.

Kathleen Cole will graduate from the Fine Arts Center in Greenville, SC in the spring of 2013. She is the current fiction editor of *Crashtest*, an online literary magazine publishing high school authors begun by her creative writing class in 2010. There is a future, and she is in it.

Dylan Combs graduated from high school in 2012. He is 5'3", dislikes long-term familiarity, and thinks it's better to be sorry than safe.

Tom Costello is a 2012 graduate of Hastings High School in Hastings, NY. He's performed slam poetry at the Apollo Theater, the Nuyorican Poet's Cafe, and the Bowery Poetry Club, and has had his writing published in 'The April Reader' and 'Teenink.' Find his poetry at http://hellopoetry.com/-tom-costello and his music at http://soundcloud.com/wisdumbrap.

Emily Sheera Cutler is a 2012 graduate of Indian Springs School in Birmingham, AL. Her works has appeared in *Chicken Soup for the Soul: Teens Talk Middle School* and journals including *CICADA*, *Aura Literary Arts Review*, and *Able Muse Review*. Her short plays have received accolades from the Alabama Writers' Forum, the Alabama Shakespeare Festival, and Young Playwrights Inc. This year, Emily was nominated for a Pushcart Prize, and she was named a YoungArts finalist in Writing for 2012.

Contributors' Bios

Katia Diamond will graduate from Westwood High School in Mesa, AZ in 2014. She spends her days mostly barefoot, drinking heinous amounts of coffee and writing. She sings more than she speaks and dances more than she walks. And is honored to be published in *Polyphony H.S.*

Kevin Emery is a 2012 graduate of the Fine Arts Center in Greenville, SC.

Clara Fannjiang thanks Ephesians and Carolyn Forchés masterpiece "The Lightkeeper" for kindling the spirit she now writes by: to rear each poem as its own pulsing, fluttering form of life, like the twist and crinkle of light through water. She graduated from Davis Senior High in Davis, CA this spring, and heads to Stanford in the fall to study computer science and linguistics. She plans to spend the rest of her life neck-deep in research, unraveling the mysteries of linguistic structures through mathematics.

Anna Feldman will graduate in 2013 from William Fremd High School in Palatine, IL. She wrote this piece a long time ago, and is glad to say she's in a much better place now.

Lya Ferreyra graduated from Rye Neck High School, in Mamaroneck, NY in 2012. Throughout high-school she has pursued her passion for creative writing and hopes to one day enter the publishing industry as a literary agent or editor.

Lillian Fishman recently graduated from Weston High School in Weston, MA as a member of the Class of 2012. Her work has been recognized in the 2012 Scholastic Art & Writing Awards and published in *The Blue Pencil*. She particularly loves Virginia Woolf, Michael Cunningham and Colum McCann.

Phoebe Goldenberg is a 2012 graduate of Cape Cod Academy in Osterville, MA.

Gabriella Gonzales' work has been published in City College of New York's 39th Poetry in Performance anthology, and her poetry was recognized on the regional and national levels in the Scholastic Art and Writing Awards. Currently, Gabriella attends Bard High School Early College in Manhattan. She will graduate in 2014.

Rebecca Greenberg is a rising junior at the Wheeler School in Providence, RI, and will graduate from high school in 2014. Writing being her primary interest, she is the editor of her high school's newspaper, *The Spoke*, and writes for the all-school alumni magazine, the *Now & Then* in addition to leading a poetry club.

Rocio Guenther graduated in 2012 from The American School Foundation of Guadalajara, in Guadalajara, Jalisco, Mexico. "Coconuts" received a regional gold key from The Scholastic Art and Writing Awards. This fall she will attend Trinity University in San Antonio, TX. She plans on majoring in English with a minor in Creative Writing.

Contributors' Bios

Stephanie Guo (Canyon Crest Academy, San Diego, CA; Class of 2014) is the recipient of the Adroit Prize in Verse, first in the *Claremont Review* Poetry Contest and four National Medals from the Scholastic Art and Writing Awards. Her work has also appeared in the *Apprentice Writer, Aerie International, Hanging Loose,* and the *Front Porch Review.*

Caroline Hamilton, class of 2014, studies Creative Writing at the Fine Arts Center in Greenville, SC with Sarah Blackman. She has received a Silver Medal for Poetry and a Gold Medal for Flash Fiction from the Scholastic Art and Writing Awards. This is her first publication.

Jonah Haven is an emerging American composer. He attended the Walnut Hill School for the Arts in Natick, MA, and graduated in 2012. As a composer he has been recognized by many competitions: the 2011 Jack Kent Cooke Young Artist Award and the 2011 NYAE Young Composers' Competition among others. Jonah's poems have appeared in *The Blue Pencil Online*. He will attend the Oberlin College and Conservatory in the fall of 2012.

Raven Hogue graduated Oak Park River Forest High school in Oak Park, IL in 2012. "Yazoo City" is a testament to my memory of my great grandfather. I had heard tall tales about his strength and met him at his weakest.

Michelle Jia is a Canadian writer/musician who lives for paper mail, summer storms and uncharted land. Her poetry has appeared or is forthcoming in *The Claremont Review, Poetry Breakfast* and *The Adroit Journal*. She graduates this year from both Markham District High School and the glorious town of Markham, Ontario.

Jordan Kincaid is a 2012 graduate of Clarkston H.S. in Clarkston, MI.

Lilian Kong goes to Wheeler School in Providence, RI. She is inspired by many writers and artists, especially poets Linda Opyr and Gary Margolis, whom she met recently at the NEYWC conference. Lilian is also a proud Chinese-American who will always love East Asian culture. She will graduate in 2014.

Joanne Koong currently lives in Irvine, CA. She is a dedicated student at the Orange County High School of the Arts (Class of 2013) where she studies Creative Writing. She has crazy awesome dreams for the future that include writing, traveling, volunteering, chess, people-watching, philosophy in late-night cafes, and living.

Peter LaBerge will graduate from Greens Farms Academy in Westport, CT in 2013. He has been published in *Gargoyle Magazine, The Blue Pencil Online, The Claremont Review,* and the *Yale Journal for Humanities in Medicine*. He received the 2012 Elizabeth Bishop Prize in Verse and two Scholastic awards. He is the founder and Editor-in-Chief of *The Adroit Journal*.

Contributors' Bios

Jane Ligon lives in Spokane, WA. She attends Lewis and Clark High School and will graduate in 2014. She writes poetry and short prose.

Anjie Liu is a junior at New Hartford Senior High School in New Hartford, NY. She enjoys reading, painting, playing the violin, and using the Internet, and plans to travel the globe with someone very special after her studies and do something nice for the world.

Maggy Liu will graduate from Saratoga High School in 2013. Her work has been published by *The Writer's Slate* and *YARN*. When she is not frolicking with Leonidas, her golden retriever, Maggy can be found reading about women's history or drawing cartoons.

Gabe Lunn is born of the Rocky Mountains but resides most of the year in Victoria, BC at Saint Michael's University School (SMUS) in its boarding houses. While inside the brick walls of his room, he has spent countless hours reading, writing, listening, playing, and experiencing many forms of the arts. After graduating in the spring of 2013, Gabe plans to expand his knowledge of English at the University of Victoria and see where he'll go from there.

Deborah Malamud is a rising senior at Harvard-Westlake School in Los Angeles, CA. She'll be graduating in 2013. Some of Deborah's writing has been published in *Teen Ink* and her school's writing magazine, *Stonecutters*. This is Deborah's first piece to be published in *Polyphony H.S.*

Kathleen Maris is student at the Fine Arts Center in Greenville, SC. She has won an Honorable Mention in the Scholastic contest, and was a finalist in the Nancy Thorpe Poetry contest.

Rose Miles is a rising senior at Saint Ann's School in Brooklyn, NY (Class of 2013). She enjoys writing poetry, counting stars, and performing in her school's black box theater, as well as (tacitly) knowing that her obese cat will one day save the world.

Jack Nachmanovitch graduated from Charlottesville High School in Charlottesville, VA in 2011. He submitted this poem when he was a high school senior, and somehow it slipped our grasp until this year. Jack now attends Pratt Institute for Creative Writing.

Brittany Newell is a cali girl who graduated in 2012 from Interlochen Arts Academy in Interlochen, MI. She is returning to her roots and will be attending Stanford in the fall.

Anthony Otten graduated from Lloyd Memorial H.S. in Erlanger, KY, in May 2012. He will attend Thomas More College this fall, majoring in English. He likes being in *Polyphony H.S.* He doesn't like being in high school. He's glad he's served his time.

Contributors' Bios

Yeong Seo (Sera) Park is originally from Seoul, Korea, and currently is a junior at St. Mark's School in Southborough, MA. Her favorite aspect about writing is that it empowers her with many voices, experiences, and identities. She loves music and the elderly as much as she enjoys writing poetry.

Jules Ray graduated from The Fine Arts Center in Greenville, SC in the spring of 2012. She enjoys organizing things into straight lines, loud techno music, and speaking in haiku. Jules will minor in creative writing at College of Charleston, and wants to write for *National Geographic*.

Upasna Saha attends Hunter College High School in New York City, NY, where she is part of the graduating class of 2015. In her (limited) spare time, she can be found inhaling chocolate and coffee, and bemoaning the fact that she will never meet F. Scott Fitzgerald or Leo Tolstoy.

Olivia Scheyer hails from Glencoe, IL where she attends North Shore Country Day School as a junior. She whittles away her time writing about life's most profound inquiries, involving spilled coffee, Spanish class, and what exactly hot dogs are made of. When she graduates in 2013, she hopes to permanently hunch over a desk studying creative writing in college.

Maia Silber is in the class of 2013 at Hendrick Hudson High School in Montrose, New York. She enjoys literature, politics and art. Maia is editor-in-chief her school newspaper and aspires to a career in journalism or publishing. She also works part-time as a reading tutor and volunteers at Hudson Valley Hospital.

Rachel Stone is the heir to the throne of a small, foreign monarchy, and enjoys flaunting her diamonds and throwing extravagant balls. As well, Ms. Stone has been published in *A Clean, Well-Lighted Place* and *scissors and spackle* literary magazines, something she enjoys reminding people of when she forgets how to use can-openers. She will graduate from the Latin School of Chicago in 2013.

Margaret Sullivan will graduate from York Suburban High School in York, PA in 2013. She is an alumna of the Iowa Young Writers' Studio and her fiction has also been published in the *Claremont Review*. Margaret is the founder and editor-in-chief of her school literary magazine, *Yourstory*, which she shamelessly plugs at every opportunity.

Lila Thulin has loved words ever since she could sound them out on her own. She lives in Utah and is a proud member of the class of 2013 at Rowland Hall, where she participates in Creative Writing, dance, and theatre.

Hannah Toke graduated in 2012 in Greenville, SC from the Fine Arts Center for creative writing. In 2011, she won a Scholastic Gold Medal in poetry and was a winner in the Nancy Thorpe Poetry Contest after several concentrated years of writing about the south and all its weeds.

When she isn't writing, **Julia Tompkins** enjoys singing, photography and African Dance, sometimes all at the same time. It can get rather hectic. She lives in Brooklyn, NY where she attends the Saint Ann's School, Class of 2014. This is her second appearance in *Polyphony*.

Laura Wanamaker is from Chatham, Cape Cod. She graduated from Walnut Hill School for the Arts in 2012 and will attend Hampshire College in the fall. She loves cold saltwater, moths, and vegetables.

Madelyne Xiao is a member of the class of 2014 at Urbana High School in Ijamsville, MD. Madelyne enjoys reading, writing, and watching old movies in her spare time. She's been on an Ayn Rand kick for the past few months. In addition, she is the founder and editor-in-chief of *Vademecum Magazine*.

Lylla Younes will graduate from boarding school at the Louisiana School for Math, Science, and the Arts in Natchitoches, LA in 2013. She enjoys swimming, debating, and writing, and she considers herself an oddball kind of comedian. She would love to go back in time and dine with Ernest Hemingway. Her future holds pizza, promise, and engineering.

Anran Yu will graduate from Desert Vista High School in Phoenix, AZ in 2013. She began writing poetry in third grade, but it took until my junior year to decide that she wanted to try to seriously get her work published.

Tina Zhu is a rising senior who will graduate reluctantly in 2013 from Shanghai American School in Shanghai, China; she is partial to polka dots, Pokemon, and Pennsylvania, and has a penchant for run-ons & a passion for poetry.

Editorial Staff 2011-2012

Executive Director
Elizabeth Keegan

Co-Founder/Managing Editor
Billy Lombardo

Print Design
Tamara Fraser

Editors-in-Chief
Clara Fannjiang
Oly Huzenis

Asst. Editor-in-Chief
Hedy Gutfreund

Dir. of Editorial Development
Keely Mullen
Mehr Singh

Advisory Board
Stuart Dybek
Jennifer Egan
Betsy Franco
James Franco
Chang-rae Lee
James McManus
Gary Shteyngart
Scott Turow

Executive Editors
Julia Aizuss
Hayun Cho
Allison Light
Annie McDonough
Sejal Jain
Olivia Scheyer
Vidushi Sharma
Rachel Stone
Ian Spear

Staff

Genre Editors	Second Readers	First Readers
Julia Aizuss	Emma Arett	Elena Abascal
Amy Balmuth	Margot Babington	Surabhi Balachander
Laura Barker	Amber Brown	Esha Bansal
Hannah Bottum	Lily Cao	Camara Brown
Hayun Cho	Hannah Chow	Emily Burns
Hanna Cunningham	Caroline Chu	Andrew Collins
Tina Czaplinska	Samantha Cohen	Courtney Cook
Alexa Fifield	Teddy Cohn	Jenny Davis
Phoebe Goldenberg	Miya Coleman	Nik Dhingra
Ioana Grosu	Jack Flynn	Erica Guo
Stephanie Guo	Kathryn Garrett	Caroline Kaplan
Sejal Jain	Kate Guynn	Kent Keller
Cindy Ji	Erin Healy	Rebecca Kirtley
Afrodite Koungoulos	Shireen Mathews	Joanne Koong
Allison Light	Gianna Miller	Brianna Lavelle
Maggy Liu	Dorothy Moore	Sarah Mania
Annie McDonough	Colin Nishi	Sarie Monieson
Kristina Mensik	Catie Rose Pate	Annie Murnighan
Mary Jane Porzenheim	Jacob Pharoah	Will Nuelle
Syeda Quader	Christina Stella	Olivia O'Sullivan
Olivia Scheyer	Kevin Ward	Ellen Pham
Vidushi Sharma	Blaike Young	Christina Piazza
Rachel Stone		Michelle Santos
Ian Spear		Aidan Sarazen
Margaret Sullivan		Hannah Srajer
Jessica Tannenbaum		Talin Tahajian
Olivia Valdes		Emily Yankowitz
		Hannah Wilson

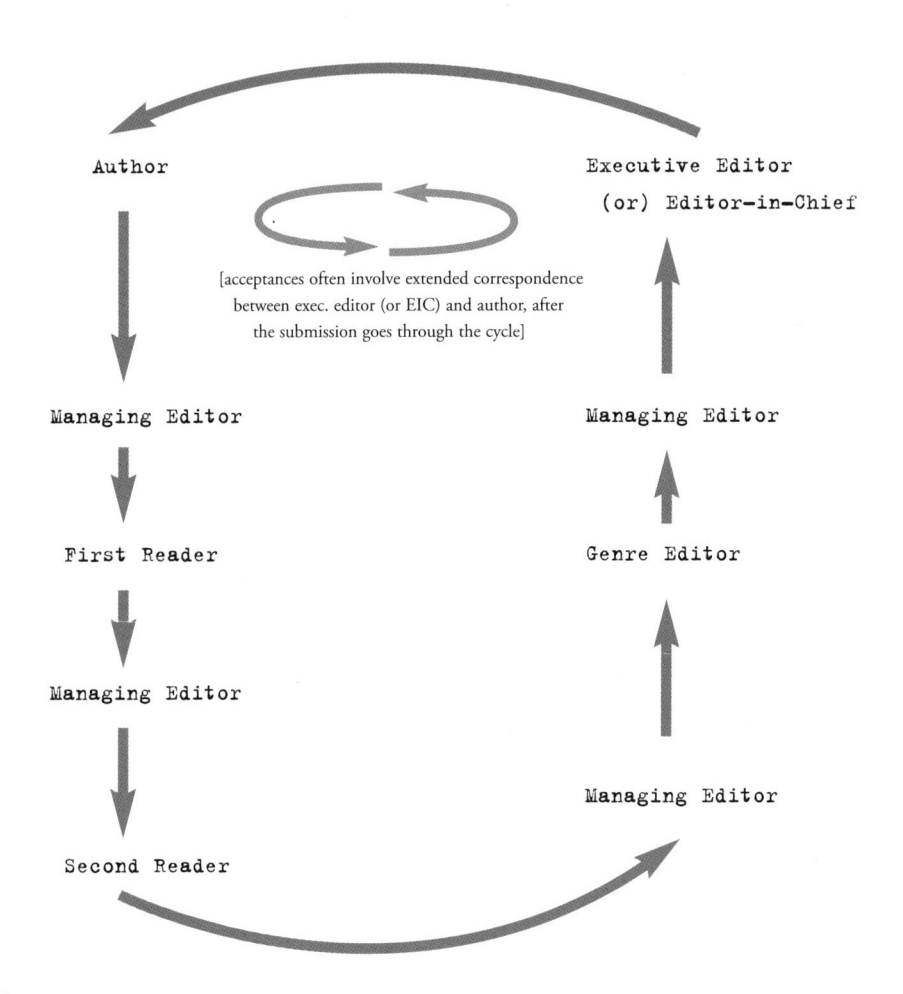

```
        Author                          Executive Editor
                                       (or) Editor-in-Chief

           [acceptances often involve extended correspondence
            between exec. editor (or EIC) and author, after
                 the submission goes through the cycle]

    Managing Editor                     Managing Editor


     First Reader                         Genre Editor


    Managing Editor


                                         Managing Editor

     Second Reader
```

Polyphony H.S.
Editorial Pipeline

All submissions (if sent in by the early deadline), whether accepted or rejected, go through this editorial cycle. The Managing Editor merely forwards the pieces. Second readers, genre editors, executive editors, and the editor-in-chief are responsible not only for editing and commenting on the submisison, but for editing the commentary of the readers and editors before them as well. Most acceptances go through an in-house editorial process. In these cases the Editor-in-Chief or an executive editor works with the poet/author before coming to an agreement on the final version of the submission.